A MEMOIR OF ABUSE, ADDICTION, SEX WORK, AND RECOVERY

OVERCOME
AMBER VAN DE BUNT

aka Karmen Karma

A BARNACLE BOOK
RARE BIRD BOOKS
LOS ANGELES, CALIF.

THIS IS A GENUINE BARNACLE BOOK

A Barnacle Book | Rare Bird Books
453 South Spring Street, Suite 302
Los Angeles, CA 90013
rarebirdbooks.com

For more information, address:
A Barnacle Book | Rare Bird Books Subsidiary Rights Department
453 South Spring Street, Suite 302
Los Angeles, CA 90013

Set in Dante
Printed in the United States

10 9 8 7 6 5 4 3 2 1

Publisher's Cataloging-in-Publication Data
Names: Bunt, Amber van de, author.
Title: Overcome: A Memoir of Abuse, Addiction, Sex Work,
and Recovery / Amber van de Bunt a.k.a. Karmen Karma.
Description: First Hardcover Edition | Genuine Barnacle Book |
New York, NY; Los Angeles, CA: Rare Bird Books, 2019.
Identifiers: ISBN 9781644280133
Subjects: LCSH Bunt, Amber van de. | Stripteasers—United States—
Biography. | Motion picture actors and actresses—United States—
Biography. | Mothers and daughters. | BISAC BIOGRAPHY &
AUTOBIOGRAPHY / Personal Memoirs. | BIOGRAPHY &
AUTOBIOGRAPHY / Entertainment & Performing Arts
Classification: LCC PN2287.B86 B86 2019 | DDC 792.7/028/0924—dc23

To my daughter, Vienna,
for giving me strength before you were even born.

Everything in this memoir is one hundred percent true as I remember it. Names and businesses have been altered for privacy.

Small-Town Girl

EVERYONE ELSE MY AGE had been planning what college they would attend, what their major would be. I never even bothered. While my classmates were Googling "colleges in Michigan," I was doing searches for "sexy stripper names." I earned the reputation of the class slut by the time I had entered sixth grade. I knew the power of sexuality and that I was interested in pursuing it. I had always craved a different type of lifestyle, and once I was eighteen, I was ready.

I wanted to be a sex worker.

Growing up in the middle of nowhere was probably beneficial for my troubled mind, but I always yearned for more. The small Midwest town of Houghton, Michigan, had no mall, no clubs, no entertainment, nothing to do. As a teenager, weekend excitement mostly consisted of getting drunk in the Walmart parking lot with the other bored teenagers.

From a young age, it was clear that I was not meant to stay a small-town girl. Girls dressing slutty, doing drugs, and partying in sweaty nightclubs without a care in the world—I'd seen this in movies, and it all appealed to me. I knew I would never experience any of those things if I settled and stayed in Michigan. Besides, I'd already had sex with all of the attractive (and even some of the not-so-attractive) boys in my town, and all of the girls already hated me either for sleeping with their boyfriends or because they were scared I was going to. It wasn't like I had friends to lose.

It was time for a change of scenery.

My dream was to become a porn star, but I decided to start small, and web-camming had always seemed like the logical place to start. To this day I still can't remember how I even found out about it, but I know I was seventeen. And when I found out I could stay home in bed and make hundreds of dollars per day, you bet I signed myself up. Of course, the camming sites denied me because I wasn't eighteen, the legal age to be naked on the Internet, but I've always been a rule breaker and a go-getter, so I came up with my own way to do it.

I decided if I went on free camming sites and teased everyone to the point that they were begging to see me naked, they would fork over some cash to actually see a show. Which is exactly what they did. After dancing around my room in front of my laptop for five minutes, I put out a message saying:

"If you want to see more, add me on MSN Messenger: princess0carmen@live.com! PAY 4 PLAY."

The amount of men I had lined up to do webcam shows for was shocking. I scheduled them back to back and performed for hours in my room until I was physically exhausted. It gave me such a rush of adrenaline doing something I wasn't supposed to be doing, but also a sense of power from being able to make money solely off my body. I refreshed my PayPal account. It jumped from the zero-dollar balance from before my hours of camming to over five hundred dollars. I was astonished to have earned that much by doing, in my opinion, pretty much nothing.

From that day forward, I laughed at the thought of working minimum-wage jobs or being a broke college student. I started logging on everyday to perform shows from my bedroom, and I couldn't believe how quickly my bank account balance was growing.

Once I turned eighteen, I signed up for every site I could possibly find. Everything was going picture perfect until the day my dad walked in on me doing a webcam show. We lived in an old house that had no locks on the bedroom doors, but since my family never bothered me, I didn't give it a second thought. Little did I know my dad would barge in on me while I was naked for strangers to watch.

"Get dressed and get in my room," my dad demanded as he marched from my bedroom doorway.

I wanted to run out of the house and never come back, but I knew I had nowhere to run to. I walked into my dad's room, and he was livid. Supposedly, I had been hacked. A pervert from Canada who was watching my webcam show tracked my IP address, which led him to finding my house phone number.

He called my dad and whispered creepily, "I'm watching your daughter fuck herself."

I started to consider moving as soon as possible. Not only was it mortifying to look my dad in the face, but after a year of nonstop web-camming, I was ready to move on to bigger and better things.

I figured the next step was to start stripping.

I hopped online and started researching the closest clubs, but there were none even remotely close to Houghton. I did find one about four hours away, though, in Green Bay, Wisconsin. After viewing the website and the reviews of the club, I quickly ruled it out as an option. The club was known for their older, overweight dancers and a commensurate lack of customers. That didn't match the glamorous image of a strip club I had in mind.

If I really wanted to move and start my new life, I only had one option: move to Florida to live with my mother, the woman I'd been terrified of since as early as I could remember, the woman who, when I was a child, told me she would kill me and abused me while my dad was at work. I was shocked to find myself even considering this as a legitimate option.

I always laugh when my dad tells me the story of him sitting down with me and my younger sister to let us know they were getting a divorce. Instead of us crying like he expected, I replied, "You mean we never have to see Mom again?" This was followed by us cheering in excitement, and it wasn't until he told us we would still have to see her once in a while that we broke down in tears.

Why did I have to get ripped off in the mom department? I was six when my parents got divorced, the same age I started seeing a therapist. After that therapist talked to me and my sister Jessica, she reported to the court that the only way my mother should be able to see us was under court-supervised visits. Jessica is only two years younger than me and she can remember living with our mom. My youngest sister, Amanda, was only six months old at the time of the divorce, so she has no recollection of any of our mom's behaviors.

Not having my mother be a part of my life seriously damaged me. It was painful to watch all my friends' moms help out in school or Girl Scouts. I never had a mom to dress shop with me for prom, do my hair for me, or to teach me about girly things. I dreaded every Mother's Day. It became a tradition very early for my sisters and I to make "Happy Mother's Day, Dad" cards in school. To this day, we still tell my dad "Happy Mother's Day" because he has done an amazing job being a mom and dad all in one. But nothing could change the hurt I felt inside of not having a mother who cared.

Although she scared the crap out of me and I hated her for never being there, I always longed for my mother. What did I do that made her threaten to kill me at only a few years old? Why was she always swearing and hitting me? Why did she leave her three children and never look back? There's no way someone who treated me that way could love me. And if my own mother couldn't love me, how could anyone?

I still don't know the answer, and these questions affect me to this day. I have never believed anyone would stay in my life—whether in a romantic or platonic relationship. I have subconsciously ruined every relationship I've ever had so that I can be the one who decides to leave. So that I could be the one doing the mistreating. I was permanently damaged by the pain my mother caused.

Maybe this is the root of why I've always been so promiscuous. I've always accepted any attention thrown my way. Someone wanting me—even if only strictly sexual—was still someone wanting me. In my head, that was showing me "love."

In the past, I never turned down anyone who wanted to touch me or fuck me. Someone wanting me always felt so good. Of course, I knew this wasn't real love, but it still felt nice having someone want me—even if only for a night.

I feel bad for my poor father. That woman completely ruined his credit score, was abusive to him, embarrassed him on a regular basis with her behavior, and damaged his reputation.

And then she left him alone with three daughters and too many questions.

"Why couldn't you have given us a nice mommy?"

"Why did you have to marry *her*?"

"How come we couldn't have gotten a good mom?"

It wasn't my dad's fault, but I'm sure he has put a lot of blame on himself. I don't know if I will ever truly recover from what she did to me in my childhood. I still cry in the middle of the night thinking of all the things I have missed out on, not having had a relationship with the woman who birthed me. My heart breaks a little inside every time I see a friend with their mom or someone posting online about how they could not survive without their wonderful mom. It still hurts, and it will always hurt.

Here I was, at the start of my adulthood about to ask the same woman who had already ruined my childhood if I could move into her house. One text message later and sure enough, she gave me the green light to move down to Florida to live with her, my stepdad, and my half-brother, Dominic.

When I broke the news to my dad, he was in complete shock. He didn't understand why I would ever purposely put myself in the same city as her, let alone in the same house. What my dad didn't realize was that it was my escape from Houghton. It was my chance to move to a bigger city and live wild and free.

I wasn't moving to be close to my mom. I was moving to become a stripper.

After a three-day cross-country drive, Pensacola, Florida, was my new home. Moving to Pensacola from my small hometown was an enormous change. There were bars, nightclubs, a mall, and, to my surprise, four strip clubs to choose from! I sat on my computer and researched all of the strip clubs to weigh out the pros and cons of each. Little did I know that by the time I would move out of Pensacola, I would've worked at all four.

Sammy's was the farthest away from where I was living, so that one automatically got disqualified. Escapes had the worst reviews, so that one was eliminated next. Now I had to decide between Infinity Island and Nightshade Show Club.

Infinity Island called themselves a "Rock N' Roll Titty Bar," and while I wasn't really into rock music, it seemed like a good club. Then there was Nightshade Show Club, which was known as the urban strip club out of the bunch. I loved hip-hop music and I loved black men, but being a white girl from a small town, I played it safe and decided on Infinity Island.

After driving back and forth past Infinity Island a few times, I finally got the balls to pull into their parking lot. It was an old, faded pink one-story building, and I could hear the rock music as soon as I got out of the car. Walking into a strip club for the first time, I had no idea what to expect. I considered turning around at least three times as I made my way across the parking lot.

When I opened the door, I saw a man sitting at a desk and two strippers, clearly drunk, hanging all over him. I could tell they expected a male customer to walk in the door by the way they stopped their conversation and stared at me.

"How can I help you?" the manager asked me.

"Are you hiring?" I shyly responded.

When he asked me if I was looking to be a waitress or stripper, I panicked. Maybe I should just start working as a waitress until I get comfortable with the strip club environment? I told him either.

"We're not looking for waitresses but if you want to dance, you can come here tomorrow for the night shift, seven p.m."

Stripping is what I sought out to do, so I was relieved when he made the decision for me. I asked him what to bring and he told me to bring heels, a bra, and a T-back. I had never heard the term "T-back" before and felt stupid when I had to ask him what that was. The drunk girl hanging onto the manager's arm turned around and said "this," pointing to her ass. She revealed a tiny piece of fabric, basically a G-string, that made a little "T" shape where it connected in the back. The thong was made specifically for strippers.

The girl's name was Chloe, and she was pretty intimidating. She had long brown hair, naturally big boobs, a small waist, and a perfect bubble butt. Little did I know this girl would end up introducing me to cocaine shortly down the road.

I had accomplished what I set out to do and got a job as a stripper, very easily in fact. This was my dream coming true. I walked out of the club with a smile anxious for the next night.

Naturally Sexual

Unlike many women who end up as strippers, I wasn't doing it because I had to. I wasn't even doing it for the money. I was doing it because there was something burning inside of me to express my sexuality. For as long as I can remember I have been sexual. It wasn't an act. I have always just been this way.

I remember it was summertime and I couldn't have been older than five. I walked downstairs in my one-piece swimsuit, and my grandma yelled, "What the heck is that?" pointing to my obvious stuffed top. I had shoved hair ties over my flat chest to resemble the shape of breasts.

Around the exact same age, my dad made me wear white tights in the winter underneath my long denim skirt and snow pants. I remember being secretly angry that it wasn't revealing enough. I got to school in my snow pants and winter gear to play at recess before class started. When all of my classmates and I got inside our classroom and undressed at our cubbies, I pulled down my tights as I took off my snow pants. I went to the bathroom and looked in the mirror, satisfied with my sneakiness, and hiked up my skirt to my belly button to make it shorter. *Much better.*

Then came second grade, and my sexuality hadn't shown signs of slowing down anytime soon. We were cleaning out our desks in class and I remember my friend Abigail whispering to me to come down to the floor with her. I lay down with her so she could tell me her secret.

"We should practice having sex."

Abigail must've been able to see I was very confused.

"You know, for when we're older, with boys!"

I wasn't sure what sex actually consisted of. I knew it was more than kissing, and I knew it was a taboo subject. I didn't want her to think I wasn't cool, so I agreed that it was a good idea.

It was Abigail's seventh birthday party, and as soon as I got there, Abigail told me to go to her room with her. She took out a disposable camera and told me to take pictures of her as she pulled down her underwear. I nervously took the photos, thinking about what her parents were going to say when they took this film to get developed. She grabbed the camera from me and told me to pose too, so off came my underwear and we took naked photos of each other. Seven years old, and I had just posed for my first nudes.

The rest of the party was normal until Abigail's mom went to bed. All four of us at the sleepover decided we wanted to watch *Titanic*. We got to the part where Jack draws Rose naked and one of the girls, Cassidy, had the brilliant idea to take turns drawing each other naked.

KARMEN AMBER VAN DE BUNT

"Draw my privates like a grown-up though," Abigail told Cassidy.

We all took turns getting drawn and I remember going to the bathroom with my drawing of me, complete with breasts and pubic hair, something that none of us were even close to having. I started to get a bad feeling that I was doing something wrong, and so I crumbled up the paper and flushed it down the toilet.

When I walked back out to the sleepover, I saw all the girls with their eyes glued to the television. Rose and Jack were having what we all assumed was sex. Abigail once again brought up the idea of practicing sex for when we're older and we all agreed. We paired into groups of two and dry-humped and kissed each other.

I didn't have another sexual experience until sixth grade, and again it was with another girl. Every time I would sleep at my friend Nicole's house, it was like a tradition that we would pretend we were sleeping at night and then start touching each other's vaginas. We would curiously touch each other for ten minutes and then go to sleep, never speaking of what happened the next morning.

At this point, and for many years later, I was fairly certain I was a lesbian. I talked to and dated boys, but that was only because I craved their attention. When it came to what I was turned on by, it was 100-percent women.

Maybe I was a bit scarred by what a family member did when I was younger and it caused me to be fonder of women. I remember vividly when my mom's brother, who was a teenager at the time, locked me in his room with him. I sat on the bed and cried as he stripped completely naked and jumped on the bed, penis flinging in my face. He was laughing hysterically, and I kept covering my eyes. I can't remember anything after that. I don't know if my grandma came to my rescue, if he finally let me leave the room myself, or if anything creepier happened. It's almost like my brain blocked it out. All I know is that it was traumatizing and wrong and decidedly not how I wanted to see a penis for the first time.

Middle school is when my reputation as a slut was born. I would let all the boys touch my butt in the hallways at school. Word quickly went around that I didn't care who touched my ass, and I became pretty popular. I began going to the movies with a group of four or five of the same boys every weekend, one whom was my middle school boyfriend. I would make out with him the whole movie, and every time he went to the bathroom or to get me a drink, the other boys would take turns sticking their hands down my pants.

Eighth grade was also the year I made up one of the biggest, stupidest lies I've ever told. I was at my friend Courtney's birthday party with about ten other girls from our school. We were all in her pool gossiping about boys and sex when one of the girls asked if I had ever had sex before.

Everyone knew I was spending a lot of time being groped by the boys in our grade, so I assumed that's why she was asking. I paused for a moment, not knowing how to answer.

Had I ever had sex before? *Hell no!* But with all ten girls looking at me with such interest, I lied. The second the word "yes" left my mouth, the entire pool was echoing with screams and a whole lot of questions.

Mostly they wanted to know, "What did it feel like?"

I had everyone's attention and I needed to come up with something fast. Little did they know I was a virgin just like them, and I had no idea how to describe sex.

With the most serious face I could put on, I told the group, "It feels like when you fall off a bike and scrape both of your knees at the same time."

I'm not sure why that was how I pictured it, but I'm sure I scared the crap out of some of those girls for their future sexual encounters.

After the birthday party, I didn't think much about the lie I told, but when I got to school the next Monday, literally everyone knew I'd had sex—or at least they all *thought* I had. I was getting so many questions from all the girls and was touched even more than usual by all of the boys. I knew this kind of lie was going to be hard to keep up with, but I didn't panic too much. It wasn't until my dad sat me down and told me we needed to have a talk that the panic really started to kick in.

"So you've been having sex?" is not the words you want to hear coming from your father's mouth when you are thirteen years old. Especially when you are still a virgin.

"NO! I swear to God!" I shouted back.

"Emily's mom told me you are, don't lie to me."

I couldn't believe one of these tattletales went home and told their mom on me! The worst part was that I was telling him the truth, but of course he didn't believe me. What thirteen-year-old would actually tell their dad the truth if they were having sex? I instantly regretted telling such a huge lie, but the damage was done. All of my classmates now thought I was sexually experienced, and so did my dad.

I kept up with that lie the remainder of middle school and all throughout high school. If I could take back any lie I've ever told, it would probably be that one. Nothing was more frustrating than losing my dad's trust on account of something I didn't even do.

◆◆◆

I LOST MY VIRGINITY for real about a year after my sex rumors floated around school. I dated my high school boyfriend, Justin, for about nine months or so before we finally decided to have sex. It was late spring in Michigan and his family had a tent set up in their front yard. We snuck in there to fool around one weekend afternoon. I was so nervous to lose my virginity, but I felt like I was ready. Plus, everyone already assumed I was having sex, so I might as well be doing it.

So right there in his front yard, he popped my cherry. Meanwhile his dad mowed the lawn around us having no clue we were inside of the tent. I vividly remember looking down and the sun shined directly on his penis—his blood-covered penis! I was horrified and stopped having sex instantly. We didn't do it again for another month or so because I was so terrified.

I stayed with Justin for almost five years, from the summer going into high school until half a year after we graduated. He was a really good boyfriend to me and I was a really shitty girlfriend to him. Although I was faithful to him the first couple years, it was mostly because I was so wrapped up in my eating disorder.

I was diagnosed with anorexia nervosa with bulimic tendencies at fourteen. My dad brought me to an outpatient program when I lost thirty pounds in a matter of months. During the worst of my eating disorder, I was fasting for five days straight, consuming only water, coffee, chicken broth, and vitamin C tablets. Whenever I would break my fasts, it would turn into a disgusting binge. I would make Justin drive me to McDonald's, then Taco Bell, then devour his family's pantry before spending at least an hour purging. The bathroom was downstairs and his mom always sat in the kitchen chain-smoking cigarettes. She knew all about my eating disorder, and I knew she would rat me out to my dad if she heard me puking in her bathroom. So instead, Justin would play Xbox Live with me five feet away, casually barfing into his garbage can. That was completely normal to us. Soon, his mom found out I was puking in his garbage so she took it out of his room, and I resorted to puking into bowls or into his towels if I was desperate.

When I was in tenth grade, I decided to go to prom—just not with Justin. Boys could only go to the prom if they were a junior or senior; however, girls could go as early as ninth grade—as long as an older boy asked them. I can't remember whether Justin had cared at all or had asked me not to go, but I don't think it would have mattered if he did. I still would've gone.

After the prom was over, I decided to go with a different boy—not my prom date—to the after-party. We were in a log cabin in the woods for maybe three minutes before the boy asked if I wanted to "go hook up in his car." I agreed, not knowing what exactly was going to happen. He sat in his back seat and immediately put on a condom, and that was the first time I cheated on someone. I had him drive me to my boyfriend's house afterward.

I woke Justin up to tell him I had slept with someone else. It was almost like I wanted to brag to him. I didn't even think he would be mad at me because I always got what I wanted, and he was very laid-back. I think that was mainly due to the fact he didn't even want to date me anymore but felt like he had to because any time he talked of breaking up with me, I threatened to kill myself. Justin was upset that I had cheated on him for a couple of hours, but we never talked about it again after that. (The whole school sure did, though...)

I didn't cheat on him again until senior year came along. This time with one of his best friends, Michael. I wish I could even remember how the whole thing got started between us, but it lasted for a good six months. Justin was completely aware that I was having sex with Michael but he never broke up with me for it.

It's so weird to think back on now, but it was basically like I had two boyfriends and both boys knew their roles. Justin knew I was having sex with his friend, but we still dated like nothing else was going on, and I hung out with him almost constantly. Michael knew I was in a serious long-term relationship with Justin and wasn't planning on leaving him, but he was still obsessed with me. He would even shoplift diet pills and vodka from Walmart just to please me. I would spend a Friday or Saturday night getting completely wasted with Michael, and then the next morning I'd have him drop me off at Justin's house. Michael ended up falling totally head over heels for me. I would tell him I loved him, but I didn't actually have any feelings for him. I just liked his attention and wanted to continue with the exciting love triangle we had going on. I took Michael's virginity and to him that was a big deal. He told me he wanted to marry me. That was way too much for me to handle—plus, I wanted to marry Justin—so eventually we broke off the fling. He was heartbroken for years about it, even confessing his love for me five years later at a bar.

Poor boy. Both of them.

After graduation, Justin and I decided to take a year off between high school and college to decide what we wanted to do. I saw my entire future with that kid, even though I sure as hell did not act like it. I was devastated when one day Justin stopped answering my calls.

I think I called him over seven hundred times in the course of those forty-eight hours, maybe more. He finally got the courage to tell me he was breaking up with me, something he probably should've done years before.

I don't know whether he was sick of my cheating, my eating disorder, or my controlling behavior. Maybe it was the fact I had accidentally stabbed him when I was furious about him liking another girl's Facebook status. Whatever the reason, he was serious and he stuck to it. Now I was the heartbroken one.

I sat in my room and refused to leave for weeks on end. Justin, being the great guy he is, would stop over every week or so and drop off some fruit and some magazines because he knew I wasn't leaving my bedroom. After a month of sulking, I started to get back into webcamming and quickly made my decision to move to Florida and start a new life. I was tired of obsessing over where Justin was and living in the same small town as him.

I was ready to run away and be a stripper.

One-Dollar Bills

I HAD JUST BEEN hired at Infinity Island the night before, and I was anxious to start my dream job. The only problem was that I had no idea what to wear. I didn't have any actual stripper heels, so I packed a high pair of black heels I already owned. I searched through my underwear drawer trying to find something that resembled the T-back they wanted me to wear. The closest thing I owned to that was a black lace thong that would have to do. I grabbed a bra-and-panty set I already owned and figured it'd be perfect to wear for my first night.

I knew I probably should've gone to a sex store and purchased actual stripper wear—panties, shoes—but I didn't want to spend the little money I had. I planned on buying all new things with the money I earned my first night dancing.

Whenever I imagined my life as a stripper, I pictured something glamorous. I couldn't believe tonight was the night I would finally get to live it. I walked into Infinity and signed in for the night shift. (I learned quickly that you never wanted to be a day-shift girl. That usually meant you weren't hot enough to work nights.) After signing in at the front desk, I took my first steps into the club. It was the first strip club I had ever seen in person. There was a girl dancing on stage with no one paying her any sort of attention—the few customers were all sitting at the bar, facing the opposite direction of the stage. It seemed a little odd, but I figured it would be busier later in the night.

The manager told me to get ready for the night, and I made my way to the dressing room, which was far from what I expected. It was more like a large closet than anything. There was a small bathroom with a toilet barely connected to the floor along with some lockers and a dirty mirror.

I squeezed past a bunch of strippers whom I could feel were staring me up and down. There were about twenty small lockers already occupied, and with maybe two feet of room to move and get changed in front of the giant mirror, I started to feel insecure.

I hated the feeling of being the "new girl," so I didn't make eye contact with anyone. I figured if I just minded my business that everyone would leave me alone. That lasted a good thirty seconds, until one of the girls asked who I was.

I told the girls my name was Karmen and it was my first night dancing. No one said anything. Without hesitation, I had picked the same name I used when I was web-camming. At this point I had already been going by Karmen for two years. I'd debated between Aubrey and Carmen, but eventually settled on Carmen. It wasn't until I started seriously considering doing porn that I knew I would need a last name. I loved the way

Carmen Karma sounded, but I didn't like how the C and the K looked. I made the obvious choice and changed Carmen to Karmen. I wasn't sure if I was actually ever going to do porn at that point, but I used it on my camming sites in the meantime.

I started changing into my stripper outfit for my first night of dancing when one of the girls seemed genuinely concerned about what I was wearing. It turned out that T-backs weren't just something random my manager wanted me to wear for no reason—they were mandated by law. Legally there had to be one inch of fabric covering your hoo-ha. T backs held your lady bits in perfectly.

The panties I brought were lace—basically see-through— and therefore not allowed in the club. Who knew strippers had so many rules? She informed me I would just have to keep my boy-shorts on all night—which was the next thing she started critiquing me on.

"Is that all you brought? That's not really a stripper outfit."

Although she said it in her nicest voice, I felt like I was being personally attacked.

I glanced around the locker room to see all of the other girls had on strappy one-pieces or shiny bikini outfits. My cotton bra was an ordinary bra any girl would wear under her clothes. My panties weren't the sexiest things in the world, either. Thoroughly embarrassed, I quickly put on my black heels, praying she wouldn't ridicule me about my shoes next.

Once dressed, I wasn't sure what I was supposed to. I awkwardly walked out of the dressing room and slowly did laps around the club, trying to seem like I wasn't nervous. Thank god two of the girls came up to me to explain what the night was going to entail. Their names were Bubbles and Georgia (clearly stripper names), and they helped teach me the ropes my first couple of weeks at Infinity Island. Bubbles and Georgia were both very "normal"-looking to me. They seemed more like the kinds of girls who would be working at a mall, not a strip club.

They eagerly took turns explaining the night to me and what I should expect. I learned that at the start of night shift, we would do "roll call" and we would repeat it once every hour. I didn't think it would be too bad since it only lasted the duration of one song.

My problem was that most of the time, the DJ played the same annoying rock song. That got old fast. During roll call, all of the strippers would hit the stage and stand in place shaking our asses, fake-smiling at the customers. It felt like cattle being herded, all twenty of us girls being yelled at to get on stage each hour on the hour.

During the first roll call of the night, the DJ would introduce us all by name and tell the guys it was going to be a "great night with titties and beer." Hearing my name over the club speaker for the first time made it finally seem real that I was actually a stripper. Ever since I knew what strippers were, I knew I wanted to be one—and here I was. My first night of all eight roll calls, I spent my time on stage observing the other girls while trying my best to look confident.

I learned Bubbles and Georgia liked to use this time to get on the stage floor and stretch provocatively. The rest of the girls either fought over the two poles or got down on the stage with their asses shaking toward the customers. Some stood still, not doing anything but looking clearly bored out of their minds. Mostly, I tried my best just to stay out of everyone's way.

Once the roll call song was over, the strippers would all push past each other and race to each customer, asking, "Want a table dance?"

Table dances were something I hated. They lasted one or two songs after every roll call, and it mostly required you to stand in front of the customer and dance for a good minute while putting your bare breasts in his face. At the end, you pulled out your thong string toward them, which in stripper language meant "give me your money" but only seemed to translate into a dollar or two. It seemed pointless to me to give that much show for so little. I was used to making five dollars a minute on webcam, where the men couldn't touch me. One dollar in person where the guy could potentially squeeze a boob wasn't too appealing.

Unfortunately, the manager of the club didn't care what I thought. If he saw me standing around, he'd order me to go ask customers for dances. I quickly made a routine of going to the bathroom after roll call and taking as long as possible. Afterward, I would go to the bar to ask for a glass of water to try to take up the rest of the time.

That first night, I watched all of the girls dancing on stage and wondered what I'd gotten myself into. I was in dance class for eight years growing up, and I knew some sexual dance moves from webcamming, but I had never danced on a pole before. I found Georgia and told her I was nervous about it, and she told me that guys don't even care about the pole. She suggested I dance around it and not on it. I felt a little better, but as each girl took her turn on stage, I grew more and more nervous. I knew it was getting closer to my name being called.

And then I heard, "Coming next to the stage, our newest dancer, Karmen!"

Well, there was no backing out now. I walked over to the stage, carefully stepping up the stairs. It was time for my first set. A set included two songs, and during the first one you danced in your stripper outfit, and then during the second one you took your top off. The first thing I did was grab onto the pole for balance as I tried my best to seduce the small crowd. I tried to do the moves I had practiced in the mirror the night before, but doing them in heels was a lot harder than I thought. I felt a little awkward until I got down on my knees and danced on the floor. And that quickly became the routine I would do for all of my sets: a little standing up and a lot on my knees.

As each dollar bill fell on the stage, I slowly became more comfortable. By the time my set was over, the stage had a decent amount of money spread across it that I happily collected. Going back to the dressing room to count my money, I was instantly already in love with the job. I felt such a rush after getting off the stage.

My first night at Infinity Island, I performed two sets on stage and one private dance. A private dance was superior to a table dance. Instead of getting a couple dollars, you got paid at least twenty bucks to dance for one song. You would take the guy by his hand into the champagne room and proceed to tell him to take a seat, before getting topless right away and dancing much closer than you would during a table dance.

The rule our manager told us was to stay a dollar bill's distance away (six inches) from the customer's crotch at all times, but girls would always break this rule during private dances—myself included. The goal was to give the best dance you could so he was hooked to you all night, or if you were lucky, for months.

After the last roll of the night at 2:00 a.m., the manager would hold the dressing room door open for us all to go to the back while he finished kicking the rest of the customers out.

This is when shit would hit the fan.

The girls who didn't make money that night would drunkenly complain and scream about their night—or worse, they would blame other girls for "stealing their customers." Sometimes girls would fight, but not often.

I was on too much of a high from my first night to pay any attention to this. I made sure my money was safe in my bag and got dressed back into my street clothes. I thought I was allowed to leave until the girls said I had to wait to "tip out."

This was the worst part about being a stripper.

You had to wait until every (drunk) girl was dressed and ready before anyone could start tipping out. If there was drama that night, we had to wait for the manager to give us all a talk, which basically entailed yelling at us. Even though our shift ended at 2:00 a.m., we never left until at least 3:00 a.m. Once all of the girls were ready, we would form a line to pay the manager, the bartenders, the DJ, and then lastly, the bodyguard—who would walk us to our car. I was irritated at having to pay over thirty bucks just to work there, but I got used to it.

I sang along with the radio, a stack of cash next to me, on my ride home that first night. I was in love with my new job and my new life. The second I got home and into my room, I dumped the pile of dirty money on my bed to take pictures and immediately uploaded one of them to Instagram to brag about my night. I was proud of myself for going after what I wanted and I fell asleep with the biggest smile on my face.

I started working at Infinity Island four times a week. It was easy money, for just sitting around a bar and chain-smoking cigarettes all night. I was only twenty years old when I got the job, so I would sip water and fake Red Bull during my shifts. Sometimes I would sneak a flask of whatever liquor was in my mom's alcohol cabinet and drink it between roll calls. There were cameras in the corner of the dressing room, so I would have to stick my head into my locker and chug down the liquor straight to avoid getting caught. Whenever I drank, the night went by quicker and the customers seemed more attractive.

                        Amber van de Bunt

I had never been one to hold my liquor well. High school parties either ended with me blacking out or violently puking within an hour of my arrival. That's how it went every single time I drank. I wouldn't just have a shot or mixed drink like my friends; I would insist on chugging straight from the bottle. The next thing I knew, without warning, I was not able to function.

In high school I drank an entire fifth of Absolut vodka at a hockey game. I ended up making a fool of myself, locking myself in the public restroom, and kicking my principal in the face when he tried to calm me down. I can't recall even one time when I drank "normally" in my entire life. Every time I drank, I drank to get trashed.

If I had never started drinking regularly, I would've made an amazing stripper. The first couple weeks I was making so much money and would actually focus on work. Once I started partying, things took a change and my priorities shifted. I was about to have my life changed in Pensacola. I would be introduced to certain people and things that would change my life—for the worst.

Two Pink Lines

W HEN I MOVED TO Florida and started my job at the
strip club, I decided I needed to find people to hang
out with. I went to Infinity Island's Facebook page and started
friend requesting some of the strippers. I would then go to their
Facebook profiles and start sending friend requests to all the
attractive guys and girls I could find.

Everyone started accepting my friend requests, and I got a
lot of private messages from people asking who I was. I would
introduce myself as new in town and we would have a generic
conversation that we should "totally hang out sometime."

The first person I took up on this offer was a guy named
Ryan. Most of the girls and guys I messaged were friendly and
said they would see me around town, but Ryan was different.

He didn't ask me to hang out—he told me we were *going* to hang out.

"How come I don't know you?"

"I just moved here from Michigan!"

"I'm going out tonight, I'll pick you up. Address?"

That is exactly how our first conversation went.

I clicked on his profile so I could scope him out before telling him yes or no. Ryan was Filipino and covered in tattoos. I had never dated an Asian guy before, but there was something about his photos that drew me to him. Each shot was of him out at the bars with groups of friends, looking like he was having the time of his life. I loved how he dressed—borderline thuggish, always wearing baggy pants and a snapback—and quickly made a judgment call that he had to be a good guy. I gave him my address and spent hours finding the perfect outfit for the night.

The only other time I had met someone from the Internet was when I hooked up with a man named Daniel. We went on a few dates that would end with us having sex in the back of his car before he would drop me off at home. A few months later I found out he had been married the whole time. But I wasn't going to let that bad experience stop me.

As the clock ticked closer to Ryan picking me up, I grew more nervous each second. He let me know around 8:00 p.m. that he was on his way with his friend Brandon, and I felt a sense of relief. With Ryan's friend with him, I figured it would be less awkward.

"You smoke?" was the next text he sent me.

Did I actually smoke? No. Did I tell him I did? Yep.

The few times I had smoked pot in my life, I ended up miserably regretting it. Marijuana and I did not mix. Each time I would become instantly paranoid and think I was dying. Sometimes I would think my arm was legitimately falling off while other times I would think I was having a genuine heart attack.

I never had fun smoking pot, so why did I tell him yes? I didn't want him to think I wasn't cool. He told me Brandon had "good shit" in the car I could smoke on the way to the bar. I just hoped this time I would be able to handle the weed.

I took a few swigs from my mom's vodka in the cabinet before saying bye and going out to meet my Internet date. Ryan didn't bother getting out of the car to greet me. In fact, he didn't even really look back or talk to me while I was in the back seat. Most of the drive involved him trying to be cool talking to his friend.

I sat in the back quiet for the most part, answering questions whenever they were asked. Finally, Ryan passed me the weed and told me to smoke. I obliged. I gave it back to him and he said he didn't smoke. I felt instant regret. I was only smoking because I wanted to impress the guy and he didn't even smoke himself.

I tried to remain calm on the rest of the twenty minute drive to the bar, but five minutes later I was overwhelmed by the idea that they were actually murderers planning to kill me. I was so high I couldn't tell what they were talking about, but every time they laughed I was convinced it was because their plot to kill me was working. In my stoned, paranoid state, I had 911 ready on my cell phone in case one of them made a move to hurt me. I sat quietly the rest of the drive while the music blasted.

We pulled up to a bar called Cabanas, which would eventually end up being like my second home while I lived in Florida. All I wanted was some alcohol to wash away the high of the weed. Everything felt like it was in slow motion, but I tried my best to act natural. The last thing I wanted to do was let them know I couldn't handle two hits of pot.

Ryan got out of the car and I was surprised to see that he was no taller than I was. I didn't really care what anyone looked like, though. Mostly I was focusing on not dying. Some of the paranoia went away once we were in the bar and there were other people around who seemed to know Ryan. I couldn't be 100-percent sure, but he probably wasn't going to kill me.

It was a Tuesday night, so the only people in the bar were a group of Ryan's friends. I met two girls that night who I ended up making out and taking photos with. I was pleased to know there were girls I could kiss down here. The girls in Michigan were either unattractive or prude as hell.

Ryan ordered the bartender to get everyone a shot, and I couldn't start drinking fast enough. I would rather be uncontrollably drunk than any bit of high off weed. I took shot after shot, trying to act as natural as I could.

When Ryan asked me why I was so quiet, I told him it was just the weed. He cockily talked about how we were going to hook up after the bar. I was so high I couldn't even form sentences, and the last thing I wanted to do was have sex with someone—especially for the first time.

I hadn't been at Cabanas for even an hour before I snuck into the bathroom to call my mom. I told her I wanted to come home and that my date was short and rude. After complaining for thirty seconds about how she didn't want to drive into town, I heard my stepdad offer to come get me. Thank god I would be getting the hell out of there soon. I kept checking my phone every other minute, waiting for a text saying he was pulling up. When the text finally came through, I told everyone I had to use the phone really quick outside.

I guess I wasn't as convincing as I thought, because Ryan came out after me as I was getting into my stepdad's car. Sinking down in my seat, I tried hiding as Ryan yelled at the moving car.

A few minutes later he sent me a text message.

"Too bad you won't be getting this, your loss," he wrote, attached to a dick pic.

Are you kidding me? I opened up the photo to see a small hairy penis and laughed about the text the rest of the night.

After that date from hell, I obviously didn't plan on talking to Ryan again. He would text me constantly, going back and forth between being nice and being rude to me. He would tell me I was missing out on the best guy in Pensacola and brag about how popular he was. I would make excuses not to see him, like telling him I worked all week. That couldn't stop Ryan.

It was a Thursday night and I was halfway through my shift at Infinity Island when in walk Ryan and his cousin. He daps up my manager and walks by, raising his eyebrow at me grinning ear to ear. Now that I wasn't high out of my mind, I could see that Ryan was definitely attractive—short, but attractive nonetheless. I pretended not to pay attention to what he was doing, but it was clear he was buddy-buddy with almost everyone at the club. He ordered shots from the bartender and took them with my boss. I went about my business, at work as usual trying my best to act natural. I knew it would be my turn on stage soon so I went to the DJ booth to pick my songs.

Deciding on what songs to choose was always difficult because I didn't know very many rock songs. I mainly chose Limp Bizkit songs for every set. I was in the middle of telling the DJ what songs I wanted when Ryan walked up into the booth. They hugged and started chatting away talking about how they haven't seen each other in a while.

"I think you'll be seeing me around here a lot more often now…isn't that right, Amber?" This guy was clearly not taking "no" for an answer.

I was partially flattered by how hard he was trying to get me but still felt cautious. Ryan must've gotten the hint that I wasn't going to be the one to initiate conversation. He sat down next to me at the bar.

"See, I told you I know everyone."

He ordered shots and snuck them to me as we talked and smoked cigarettes for the next half hour. Ryan never asked me about myself and never tried to be sweet to me. The only card Ryan knew how to play was the cocky one.

I was bored out of my mind listening to him brag about how much of a big deal he was in Pensacola. I found out later that he was known all right—but mostly for having sex with his friends' girlfriends and for running out on his bar tabs.

"So you going to come to a hotel with me after this?"

I couldn't believe how blunt he was. What I really wanted all night was to go home and crawl into bed. However, now that I had a few shots in my system, I started to debate this idea. I thought back to the unimpressive dick picture he sent me the week earlier and reminded myself there wasn't much I'd be missing out on if I just drove home.

Why did he want me to go to a hotel, anyways? Didn't he have an apartment? I had never gone to a hotel room with a guy before. The whole idea sounded like I was a hooker—except I knew the guy who couldn't pay his fifteen-dollar bar tabs was definitely not paying me for sex. I came up with countless reasons why I couldn't go with him that night. I kept reassuring him that we could hang out when the weekend came.

"Fine, well, at least come to my truck and talk to me after work," he said.

I finally agreed.

Two a.m. rolled around, and I really wasn't in the mood to do anything other than leave. My buzz had completely worn off and I was tired and hungry. Stripping sober and stripping drunk are two completely different worlds. When you're sober, you're completely exhausted, as any normal person would be in the middle of the night. When you're drunk, you don't want the night to end—you are trying to find the after-party or any other person who will stay up all night to get fucked up with you.

After tipping out, I waited for the bouncer to walk me to my car, something they did every night with each dancer. From time to time a creepy customer would wait in the parking lot and try to approach the girls, so it saved us from being harassed—or worse.

I wasn't even out of the door when I saw Ryan standing outside waiting for me. Well, there was no getting out of this one.

We walked over to his lifted navy-blue Chevy Tahoe and got inside. He turned his music up and straight-up started groping me. He didn't even try to kiss me or talk to me before sliding his hands in my pants. It had been at least a month since I'd last had sex, so I figured I might as well just go for it. We moved to the back seat and he got on top of me for maybe thirty seconds before cumming inside of me without any warning.

There is no feeling more disgusting than having a man you don't love cum inside of you. I drove home not knowing how to feel about the whole night. Sure, he was cute, but his attitude and the way he treated me were horrendous. Plus, who cums in someone they just met without even asking them first? Agreeing to have sex with Ryan that night would be the biggest regret of my life. The consequences would wind up much greater than just shitty sex.

Ryan kept up the appearances at my work, and I started to accept his asshole tendencies. I think I even found it cute at first. I would look forward to the times he would stop in because he would sneak me shots of Fireball. One night around midnight, he told me that I should leave work. I knew it was a big no-no to walk out on your shift and I didn't want to be fired.

"I'm cool with your boss. I can get you to leave early—just watch."

Sure enough, my boss agreed that as long as I tipped him out, I could leave if I wanted to this one time. Ryan told me to go change and meet him back out by the bar. I did as he told me.

We drove to Cabanas and started drinking with his friend Brandon, the guy whose weed got me fried out of my mind. It turned out Ryan had an agenda for the night. He'd kept telling me he wanted to fuck me with another guy, and I had secretly always wondered what it would be like to be with two guys at the same time but had yet to experience it. I told him I was down, but who would be the other guy?

That night at Cabanas, the look on Brandon's and Ryan's faces made it all click. They had both clearly talked about this before I had any idea what was going on.

I drank as many shots as I could stomach in preparation for the night ahead. I was nervous, but I was also turned on by the idea. We went to Brandon's house a few hours later, and Ryan brought me into the bedroom. Brandon stayed outside the room while Ryan got head from me. I don't think Brandon was sure if this was seriously going to happen or not.

"Come fuck my girlfriend," Ryan yelled to Brandon in the next room.

We'd never had that conversation before, but I was too drunk to care about Ryan calling me his girlfriend. Ryan lay down and instructed me to get on top of him. He then ordered Brandon to get behind me to fuck my ass.

"I think we should switch...seriously...I should be on bottom," Brandon warned.

But Ryan was stuck on wanting my vagina.

I soon felt why Brandon wanted to be on the bottom—he had the largest penis I had ever felt. Even with all of the alcohol in my system, I could still feel the pain of him inside of my ass. His dick was so big that it was pushing Ryan out of me.

Clearly frustrated and embarrassed about how small he was next to Brandon, Ryan told us he was going outside for a cigarette. While he angrily walked out of the room, Brandon and I kept having sex—vaginally, thank god. But less than a minute later, Ryan stormed back into the house, cursing us out and throwing things around the living room. Apparently, we weren't supposed to keep having sex, and I was supposed to have followed him outside.

He screamed at us both and started pushing me around. Brandon wedged himself in the middle, protecting me from Ryan's swings, and eventually Ryan left, slamming the door behind him.

What had just happened? I was supposed to be having my first two-man threesome with Ryan—one that *he* initiated—but it had gone very wrong. My phone kept ringing, and of course it was Ryan. Finally, against Brandon's advice, I answered. Ryan begged me to go outside to talk to him.

I walked out the apartment door and right into a hard punch from Ryan. He caught me square in the face, and I fell to the grass while I heard a neighbor scream. Brandon went running after Ryan, but by the time Brandon knew what was happening, Ryan was already in his Tahoe about to drive away. The cops came a few minutes later and I told them I didn't want to press charges. How stupid.

It was late, and so I spent the night at Brandon's house and fell asleep wondering whether or not I had actually had my first double penetration—DP for short. I'd often fantasized about doing it, but getting one to actually happen in "real life" was difficult. I had many threesomes with girls, but the next time I would get to have DP would be years later—on camera.

After the altercation at Brandon's house, Ryan wouldn't stop harassing me over text message. His messages ranged from calling me a stupid slut to using sad face emojis to telling me I broke his heart. I would remind Ryan that he had planned the whole evening, but there was no reasoning with him. He would tell me "I owed him" and that now I had to give him anal sex, along with many other bizarre sexual acts that you definitely don't "owe" anybody.

When I tried completely ignoring Ryan's texts, he would become livid and threaten to get me fired from Infinity. I wasn't sure if he could really just tell my boss to fire me and that my boss would actually listen to him—but I wasn't sure he couldn't, either. I loved my job; I just didn't love being around Ryan. And so I ignored as many texts as I could until they got too threatening.

Around that time, I became really good friends with a girl named Hayden, who also worked at the strip club with me. She had long, brown wavy hair and a skinny frame. She was a year younger than me and every bit as wild and goofy. She opened up to me about her life. Apparently, her mom worked the day shift at Infinity. She also told me she had a three-year-old baby whom her grandma took care of. These things seemed shocking to me, but it was a breath of fresh air to have someone be so honest. We became best friends almost instantly and started hanging out after work and on the weekends.

It was a Wednesday night and instead of going to work we decided to ditch and go to Cabanas instead. We knew we could always get booze there, so it would be much more fun than sitting around sober at Infinity all night. We were some of the only people at the bar, but we had the time of our lives dancing on top of the bar, making out and posing for selfies. We couldn't get the bartender to serve us shots, so we were only slightly tipsy off the couple that we could get other people to buy us.

We left Cabana's around 1:00 a.m. and I dropped Hayden off at her place. There was no point staying there until closing time if there wasn't going to be alcohol served to us. On the way back to my mom's house, I texted my sister Jessica, "Skype in 20?"

Jessi and I were only two years apart in age and grew to be best friends around high school. We did almost everything together in Michigan, so it was a hard adjustment being across the country from her. We tried to Skype each other as much as we could.

I sat gossiping with my sister about the usual. I would tell her the weird things Mom was doing, and she would tell me about college. I decided to clean out my room while Skyping with her and came across a pregnancy test.

I smiled, showing her what I found. "Should I take it?"

"Why? Do you think you're preggo?" Jessi didn't look surprised. I took pregnancy tests all the time in Michigan and they were always negative.

"No, but I just want to take it for fun!"

I peed in a cup I found on top of my dresser and dipped the test into the pee while we carried on normal conversation. Neither of us thought anything serious about the test. And then suddenly my heart sank and I instantly started bawling hysterically. Jessi kept asking what was wrong, but I couldn't stop crying to talk. I just lifted up the pregnancy test to show her the two little pink lines.

I was pregnant.

She put her hand over her mouth.

I had no idea what to do. Was I seriously pregnant? In a state of panic, I got off of Skype and woke up my mom.

She was not the type of person I would consider waking up on a normal basis—she would chew me out and ruin my day for even making a peep while she was asleep—but I was in a frenzy. Once she realized why I was waking her up, she told me to go to the urgent care once it was open so I could be certain. I sat wide-awake for five hours, waiting until I could get to see a doctor.

KARMEN AMBER VAN DE BUNT

Who was the father?

I'd had sex with both Ryan and Brandon since I moved to Pensacola, but I thought back to the first time I had sex with Ryan and when he came inside of me.

I texted Ryan for the first time in days: "YOU GOT ME PREGNANT!"

"What?" was all I got back from him. I couldn't stop sending him text after text blaming him for what had happened.

"I'm not the only one you fucked in Pensacola, it's not mine."

I couldn't believe this was really happening to me. I used to laugh and make fun of the trashy women on Jerry Springer who didn't know who their baby daddies were—now, suddenly, I was one of them!

The wait at the urgent care office felt like days. They took a urine sample and finally walked back into the patient room to tell me my results a half hour later.

"Congratulations, you're pregnant!"

I instantly broke into tears and the doctor awkwardly realized this was not a happy moment. They told me I was five weeks along. I took out my iPhone to do the math on my calendar and sure enough, it landed on the week Ryan had came inside of me outside Infinity Island.

The doctor gave me a prescription for prenatal vitamins and a nausea medication. She told me to make an appointment with my regular doctor as soon as possible to start my pregnancy appointments.

I spent the rest of the day in bed crying, debating what I was going to do. I was only twenty years old, I wasn't in a serious relationship, and I was not able to provide financially for a child. Even after showing Ryan the facts that he was indeed the father, he kept saying I was probably sleeping with other guys behind his back and that he didn't believe me.

He only spent one day denying it was his—after that is when the threats started.

"If you don't have an abortion, I'll kill you and your family."

If Ryan didn't instantly get a response from me, he would send text after text until he got a response.

"I have your fucking address, I'll come by and shoot you in your sleep. Your little brother too."

My half-brother, Dominic, was only ten at the time.

Ryan's threats scared me, but I kept them to myself. I rationalized them as all talk. I was depressed enough knowing I was pregnant, but for Ryan to be sending me death threats took my mental state to an all-time low.

My family has always been against abortion. Everyone I knew growing up in my small hometown was pro-life. People did not have abortions. You had to live with your choices and deal with the consequences. Never in my wildest dreams did I think I would be debating having an abortion of my own.

I imagined life if I kept the baby. I would be a single mother, but that didn't bother me as much as thinking about how his father would be a psychopath. Growing up myself with only one parent was very damaging. I spent my entire childhood, teenage years, and even my early twenties harming myself to deal with the pain of having an absent mother. My eating disorders, self-harm (cutting), alcohol issues, and depression were all rooted from my mother. At least, that's the conclusion arrived at by my countless therapists.

I started seeing a shrink when I was only six years old, and my dad made me continue until I was eighteen. The last thing I wanted for my child was to feel the pain I had felt. I knew Ryan would be just as bad of a parent as my mother was. Sure, I could be the best mom in the world—just like my dad was the best dad in the world, to me—but I knew from personal experience that it wouldn't be enough.

It didn't seem fair to bring a child in the world when I wasn't fit to be a parent. I had never even lived by myself; I had no idea how to be an adult, let alone a mom. I kept telling myself I could do it alone, but with Ryan's texts coming through constantly, I knew there was no way I could make this man a father. The thought was terrifying.

I skipped work that Thursday night. I was in no shape to leave my bed. I called into the club and told my boss what was going on and he completely understood. He said I could come in whenever I was ready, and I told him I would come in the next night. Regardless of whether I was going to keep this baby or have an abortion, I needed money either way.

I played "Someone I Once Knew" by Dead Celebrity Status on repeat that whole night. It was a song I used to listen to because of the eating disorder references, but now I was listening to it for a whole different reason. The song had a verse about a girl getting pregnant and being in the same situation I was in.

> She's staring at her belly, she's so scared to touch it,
> Imagining the feeling when it kicks inside her stomach.
> Too late for safe sex, should have used a latex.
> She can't afford a baby on minimum-wage paychecks.
> Her waistline climbs by inches,
> 'Cause she traded in the morning workouts for morning sickness.
> Feeling nauseous, sleeps on her back cause she's cautious.
> Give life or take life, that's her only options.
> Only if she had a magic wand, she'd go back to that night
> And put her clothes back on.
> But she can't change time, or what's growing inside.
> How could she love something that's barely alive?

Her body's aching, shaking, from sweaty palms, and cold sweat.
Mentally exhausting like phone sex.
No regrets, life or death, it's high stakes.
'Cause right or wrong, it's only her choice to make."

I would listen to the verse over and over again, weeping along with the lyrics. Never had words hit so close to home before. I didn't know how my body was still producing tears when I hadn't stopped crying in over twenty-four hours. My mom and stepdad knew I was torn between what to do, and after telling me I should keep it, they ultimately told me it was my decision and that they would be supportive either way.

Going back to work that Friday was difficult. I didn't want to be sexual when I was having such a serious dilemma in my life. I told two of the strippers I was friends with, Hayden and Chloe, that I was pregnant. Both of them suggested I look into Planned Parenthood. Chloe told me she went there before for an abortion while Hayden told me how hard being a single parent was. I knew Hayden didn't even take care of her own kid, and I absolutely didn't want to end up like that.

Both of these girls also knew Ryan from growing up in Pensacola. They knew what a horrible guy he was and had warned me about him from the start. I lit up a cigarette, something I hadn't done in days, because I knew what decision I was going to make.

I spent Saturday morning looking at the Planned Parenthood website. I felt ashamed to even be on the site, but I knew this was something I was probably going to end up doing. It said there were different types of abortions: an in-clinic abortion and an abortion pill you could take at home. After Googling both of them intensely, I decided on the in-clinic option. There was a phone number for scheduling appointments, but I just couldn't get my fingers to dial the number.

I decided to tell Ryan what he would consider "the good news." He seemed extremely relieved and told me it was about time I started thinking logically. I reminded him that he told me he would pay for the procedure.

◆◆◆

I FINALLY MADE THE call to Planned Parenthood and scheduled my abortion for the following week. I broke the news to my mom and asked her if she could be the one to drive me. The woman on the phone told me I wouldn't be able to drive myself home after being under the local anesthesia. My mom agreed.

I didn't feel like myself the week leading up to the abortion and didn't feel like myself for quite some time afterward. Abortion was not something I took lightly. I was disgusted with myself for going through with it, and every day I would start to debate if I was making the wrong choice.

Even though I had made my decision to get rid of my baby, I still had five pregnancy apps downloaded on my phone. I spent hours scrolling through the baby names app, wondering if my baby was a boy or a girl and what his or her name would be if I went through with the pregnancy. I spent my free time image-searching "half white, half Filipino babies," imagining what my little baby would look like.

It was the most heart-wrenching decision I'd ever had to make, but my gut told me this pregnancy was not something I could handle under the circumstances.

The drive to Planned Parenthood was a silent one. I considered changing my mind with each mile we drove. My mom tried to make normal conversation with me, but I couldn't fake happiness—not today. I had always heard of pro-life petitioners, and I'd seen them once in a while on the side of the street, but it took me by surprise to see a whole mob of them standing on the sidewalk that morning. It was so early that the sun had not fully risen, but here were angry petitioners camped outside—one even holding a real infant. They all yelled at me, harassed me, called me a murderer as I walked into Planned Parenthood.

Once I got through the door, I asked where the restroom was and broke down silently in a stall. I didn't know if I could go through with this anymore. I was feeling horrible enough about my decision and being called a murderer and seeing a live baby didn't make me feel any better about myself. Was I really going to go through with this abortion? There was a little peanut inside of me wanting life, wanting to grow and be loved. Then I thought about Ryan and his threats to me. I thought about the fact I had been drinking and smoking this entire pregnancy. I was here for a reason. I had made my choice, and all that was left was to go through with it.

I filled out a few pages of paperwork and was instructed to wait in their waiting room. There had to be at least twenty people in the room already. All of us were about to kill our own children. I felt disgusting being in that building. Never had I been so ashamed—which is saying a lot.

The nurse finally called my name and my heart stopped. I said goodbye to my mom and followed the nurse. She gave me a gown and shoes to change into and had me sit on a bench with the other girls dressed in gowns. One by one we were walked back into a room to seal our babies' fates.

"Amber Teliin."

It was my turn. I was called into the room I had watched the other girls enter nervously. The first thing the nurse did was give me an ultrasound to see how far along I was. She showed me that the baby's heart was beating strong—something I really couldn't handle seeing. She then asked if I wanted a picture of the ultrasound and I quickly denied. Split seconds later, I changed my mind and asked her to please print one for me. I knew I shouldn't have this picture to stare at, but I was so curious. I knew I would have always wondered what the ultrasound picture looked like if I denied it.

She handed it to me, and a tear rolled down my cheek. After showing me the baby's heart was beating and giving me a photo of the baby that I was about to kill, the nurse left and said she would be right back in with the doctor. Could I just run out now? I had already paid the six hundred dollars, but all I could picture was the little heartbeat I saw on the ultrasound screen. I was his or her mommy. Didn't I want to be a better mother than my own?

The doctor and nurse came back in and seemed in a rush. I guess he had many babies to abort that morning. The doctor was not sympathetic whatsoever, and I could tell this was just another daily task for him.

I wasn't ready but they injected me with pain meds, something I paid an extra one hundred dollars for. The next thing I heard sounded like a vacuum and the doctor spread my legs apart. He had to tell me repeatedly to stop trying to close them. It was a natural instinct to try to stop him. The nurse took initiative by holding my legs wide apart for the doctor.

It was all happening too fast and all I wanted was a second to breathe. I could tell the doctor was getting angry and impatient as he started to perform the abortion. The whole process only felt like a minute, during which I cried out loud the entire time.

When I felt him stop, I looked up to see him throwing something away in the trash can. It was my baby. I couldn't believe he just dumped it in the trash while I was right there watching. I was not okay. This whole situation was not okay.

The nurse helped me into a wheelchair while the doctor left the room without a word. I cried uncontrollably as the nurse wheeled me into the "recovery room." It was a room full of maybe ten recliners and there were five other girls in the room silently eating pretzels. The nurse helped me into the chair and gave me a small cup of pretzels. She told me I would be feeling very nauseated for the next couple of hours and that I should eat the pretzels to settle my stomach. Eating was the last thing I wanted to do.

I would regret not eating them as I threw up into a bag the entire car ride home. I hated crying in front of people, especially girls who had just gone through the same procedure I had but who were able to keep it together. But I could not control my emotions. I cried and cried while replaying the doctor throwing away a bloody mess in the garbage can. The "ding" of the metal lid slamming back down rang through my ears. My baby was now placed in a trash can among other countless dead babies.

What had I done?

◆◆◆

I LAY IN BED for the next week in a sense of shock. I had to wear thick pads to bed and sleep on a puppy pad, so I didn't stain the bed with all of the blood that was leaving my body.

It was painful, daily proof that my nightmare was indeed real. I didn't want to talk to anybody, and I wasn't sure when—or if—I would ever feel better. I heard my phone go off and it was a text from Ryan, the last thing I needed at the moment.

"I wish you never killed our baby : ("

I could not believe what I was reading. How dare he have the audacity to say those words to me? This was the same person who was sending me death threats for not wanting to have an abortion.

If he had been a supportive partner from the beginning, I might have kept the baby in the first place. Such a huge part of my decision to go through with my abortion centered on the fact that the baby would never have a father in his life. Now this same man was telling me he wanted the baby now that it was gone?

My heart was broken beyond repair. I knew Ryan was most likely lying to make me feel bad about my choice, but how could someone be so heartless? I was absolutely appalled at how manipulative he truly was.

Making the decision to have an abortion was what I thought was the best decision for me. However, getting rid of the baby inside of me didn't mean I would get rid of the depression surrounding the situation. I had always dealt with depression, diagnosed when I was fourteen years old, but this was a sort of pain I had never endured. It felt like something was missing. I felt empty. I felt worthless.

All I could think about late at night as I was trying to fall asleep was how I had killed my own child. I drove myself insane replaying the moments of the abortion in my head. I started to think I had made the wrong decision, and the regret was overwhelming.

Little did I know I would soon be finding a new coping method to deal with my issues.

Love At First Snort

ISUBCONSCIOUSLY BEGAN FINDING ways to numb my pain after my abortion. Of course, I knew how heartbroken I was about my decision, but I wasn't fully aware of how bad it was truly affecting me. I knew I had to move on and stop dwelling on what had happened because there was nothing in this world that could take my baby out of that trash can and put it back inside my uterus.

After taking a week off to stop bleeding, I returned to Infinity Island. I started bringing booze inside my dancer bag every single night, along with one or two stripper outfits, a pair of stilettos, perfume, makeup, cigarettes, and a flask. This was nothing unusual for a stripper bag to consist of, and while it never contained enough liquor to get me completely drunk,

I always got a nice buzz from it, which in turn helped me make friends with most of the girls at the club.

I had started work as the shy new girl, but now with the help of alcohol, I felt more like myself. Chloe and Hayden were always the main girls I would hang out with throughout the night, but I was cool with countless others. Soon there were plenty of girls newer than me and I felt like I was right at home working at Infinity Island.

Ryan stopped showing up at my work uninvited, and I could finally focus on making money instead of excuses for why I couldn't hang out with him. Things were coming back together better than ever. I was making good money and had a good group of friends. This was exactly what I was hoping for when I left Michigan to start my "new life."

A stripper's schedule (assuming she doesn't have kids) is the polar opposite of a normal work schedule. Your average stripper will get home from work around four in the morning and fall asleep around five in the morning. This means that your average stripper wakes up around dinnertime with enough time to eat, shower, and put on her whore makeup before heading to another night on the pole. I was getting ready for work one night when Chloe texted me that we should go out instead of going to work. It turns out, this wouldn't be the first or last time she would ask—and it certainly wouldn't be the last time I said yes.

Working at a strip club wasn't the same as working a normal nine-to-five job. Technically we did have four days a week that we were "scheduled" for, but it was never strictly enforced. When you first get a job at a strip club, the manager will usually come up to you with a schedule list and ask you to pick four days. You're welcome to work every day if you please, but you're supposed to always work the days you chose. This ensures that the club will always have enough dancers. Once

I saw I could get away with skipping a day here and there, it became a pattern.

Something else I found out about most strippers in the Pensacola area was that they didn't have their own vehicles. As a result, I also became a personal taxi for every stripper I made friends with. Most of the girls took cabs to and from Infinity Island, and I figured they weren't using their collection of one-dollar bills toward a vehicle. I wondered where their money was going.

It didn't take long for me to find out: straight up their noses.

We decided the first place we were going to stop that night was Live, a nightclub that Chloe and I would soon go-go dance at once per week. We would get paid a flat rate from the owner, plus we were able to drink for free all night long, so it wasn't a bad deal. Plus, I loved the attention of being one of the only girls in the club dressed in panties and a bra.

Since we technically "worked" there, we knew we would have no problem getting in without paying the cover charge. For the almost three years that I lived in Pensacola, I never paid cover once even though I went out pretty much every night.

It started like any normal night out for us: we chain-smoked cigarettes as the bartender handed us free shots. Once we had danced and drank for a couple hours, we decided to head over to Cabanas. Everyone in our "friends" group was a regular at Cabanas. And I put "friends" in quotes because I didn't talk to any of these twenty acquaintances when I wasn't drunk, but when we saw each other out, we were all best friends. I would dance with and make out with these people on a regular basis, but I didn't even know their phone numbers or last names.

Cabanas was a place you could go to dance on a bar or watch girls dance on the bars. It is what a lot of people would call ratchet. It was filled with gangster rap music and girls quick to twerk on any guy who tried them, so naturally it was my favorite place to be. I had also already slept with two of the three bartenders, and therefore the drinks were, once more, on the house.

One of the bartenders, Anthony, was the first (but certainly not last) black man I ever had sex with. He took me to the attic of the bar, which is a place I often had sex. I had also had sex with a girl named Lauren up in that attic while a group of guys watched. Lauren would end up being my roommate a year later. I'd also had sex with Ryan up there a number of times. I think those are the only people I've ever slept with in the attic at Cabana's, but as I blacked out by the end of every night, I can never be too sure.

The other bartender I slept with had a girlfriend, but I didn't let it stop me. One night, when the bar was pretty dead, he followed me into the girls' bathroom and banged me in one of the stalls. Even though he only lasted a minute, we somehow managed to break one of the hinges off the stall door. They never fixed that door, and it served as a reminder of what a slut I was every time I used their restroom.

Chloe and I were pretty decently drunk when she asked me something I had never been asked before.

"Want to share a gram of blow?"

Being from a small town where the only drug you could get your hands on was marijuana, I was taken aback. I had always imagined a person that did cocaine would be super secretive about their drug use, but Chloe was nonchalant. She used the same tone someone might use to ask if I wanted to share a pizza.

I technically considered myself a cocaine virgin at that point in my life, but there had been a time two years prior when I was also exposed to the drug. I was in Panama City, Florida, for spring break with two girls from my hometown. We went to a hotel of a famous rapper after meeting him at a club, and I had anal sex with him in front of my friends and his friend—though they awkwardly went on the balcony when they saw what was going on.

Once business was finished, the rapper and his friend started lining up coke on the dresser. All three of us were giving each other "what the fuck" looks and although we were extremely nervous, we each attempted to do a line, not wanting to seem uncool. The next thing I remember, us three girls were running toward the car as fast as we could, our heels in hands.

We were so terrified we were going to die after doing cocaine, a HARD drug. No one we had ever known had done cocaine or even had an opportunity to try it. We rushed back to our hotel room in disbelief of what we had done. I never felt the effect the first time I did coke. I'm not sure I even got any up into my nose, but I was nervous. Up to that point, my opinion of the drug was that it was deadly and a big deal. Soon it would be just as regular to me as a cup of coffee in the morning.

I told Chloe that I would share a gram with her and then waited while she went and talked to a short Asian guy that was always at Cabanas. Every time I saw him he was quietly playing pool in the back corner. Little did I know he was always there because he was a cocaine dealer.

Chloe came back and said it was going to be sixty dollars. I was mind-blown. Sixty bucks? I thought it was going to be around twenty. I clearly was not cocaine educated. I took forty dollars out of the ATM and Chloe covered the rest. She did the drug deal while I waited by the bar and panicked.

Sure, I could drink an entire fifth of vodka by myself, but cocaine was a whole other world to me. She gave a head nod and told me to follow her into the bathroom. Inside the broken stall door that I had previously ruined while having drunken sex, she took out the little baggie.

It was a clear small baggie maybe an inch tall and an inch wide. Even smaller was the amount of white powder actually inside the bag. People really shelled out so much cash for this? I felt ripped off but was focused more on what we were about to do with it. Chloe asked for my car keys and I handed them to her. I watched her put the tip of the key into the baggie and pull it back out with a small amount of powder on it.

"Plug my left nostril."

Holding the baggie and key made the ability for her to do it herself impossible. I plugged one nostril and watched the coke disappear into her other nostril. She handed me the baggie and keys—it was my turn. I imitated exactly what I had just watched her do. This time, unlike on spring break, it actually went up my nose. I could feel a dull sting as I snorted the powder. I instantly felt a high like I had never felt before.

Chloe didn't have the slightest clue that this was the first time I had ever successfully used or bought cocaine. It was the first "upper" I had ever done, and I was in love. I hated weed and pills, and now I understood it was because downers weren't my cup of tea. Cocaine gave me a feeling I can't fully explain. It was like nothing else mattered. I felt so confident and on top of the world when I used it—all of my worries would fade away while I had the time of my life.

We spent the rest of the time at Cabanas doing key bumps in the bathroom until last call. Chloe's friend, Madison, was at the bar and she invited us to come over so we could continue getting high. All three of us sat in the middle of her bed taking turns doing lines off of a *Cosmopolitan* magazine. I watched them as they cut up lines, breaking down the coke until it was fine, like the consistency of sand. I took mental notes of everything they were doing so I could replicate the process on my own. There was no question in my mind that I wanted to do this again. Once our baggie and Madison's baggie were completely empty, we smoked a few cigarettes and I drove us home.

I was always the designated driver—never sober, mind you, just designated. Ever since I got my first vehicle, I was not afraid to drive under the influence. I was eighteen when I got in my first drunk driving accident and spoiler alert: it wasn't the last.

For my high school graduation, my dad bought me a red Grand Am. This was a huge deal because I never expected my dad to buy me a car, let alone to be able to afford it. I was so grateful and excited, yet a week later the car was totaled.

I had been drinking all night when I decided to drive over to my on-again, off-again boyfriend's house. He was straight-edge and had no tolerance for the drunk me. After arguing back and forth, he told me to leave, so I got in my car and did just that.

In my head I was always fine to drive. I never thought I was "too drunk." I was driving home perfectly fine, and then the next thing I knew I was losing control of the vehicle. I thought the road turned slightly left but it really was slightly right. Correcting this mistake while going around sixty miles an hour, I spun the car out and landed upside down in a ditch.

Canal Road was known for taking many lives and I'm lucky mine wasn't one of them. I sat in shock, upside down in the pitch dark. I unbuckled and hit the ceiling of my car, which was crushed down to half its original height. I grabbed my phone to call for help, but the screen read "NO SERVICE." The only choice I had was to click the emergency call button, and I was quickly connected.

"I'm drunk. I flipped my car," I said.

Realizing I had just called the cops on myself for a DUI, I quickly hung up the phone with regret. I was such an idiot! The only way I could exit my vehicle was to pry myself out of the window. As I dragged my body out of the car, I was too drunk to realize I was dragging my body over broken glass from the window. I ran down the lightless street and called one of my good friends, Mikey, to come pick me up.

When he got there, he quickly took his shirt off to wipe off all of my blood. My right breast was completely split open, along with my left thigh. I couldn't feel anything. All I knew was that we had to leave the scene of the accident before the police came. Too late. Not even two minutes behind my friend was a police officer. They had traced my call after I hung up on them. After asking me what had happened, he took out a breathalyzer and I knew I was screwed. I was familiar with these devices because I'd already had three minor in-possession charges for being drunk at parties. I blew a 0.1 and was immediately arrested.

❖❖❖

You would think after this traumatizing accident that I would learn not to drink and drive—especially after my dad's reaction—but it didn't affect me whatsoever. I bought myself a new vehicle almost instantly. I paid for it in full with cash from all of the money I had saved from web-camming and was back to driving drunk in no time. (Over the next couple of years, if I ever thought I was too drunk to drive, I would get my hands on as much blow as possible so I was "okay" to drive.)

That first time with cocaine, I spent the night at Chloe's house and never mentioned to her I was now obsessed with the drug. Lying in her bed while she was fast asleep, all I could focus on was the fact that I wanted more and more. I didn't feel tired. In fact, I felt as though I could party for another twenty-four hours. With the cocaine in my system, I stopped reminiscing about killing my baby and could finally escape all of my issues. It wasn't until the sun came up some hours later that I finally got my brain to calm down so I could get some sleep.

The next day I decided to stop at Cabanas before my shift at Infinity Island to see if I could buy some cocaine from the mysterious Asian by the pool tables. Sure enough, he was there and he agreed to sell me a gram. He was hesitant at first because he had no idea who I was, but after telling him I was a friend of Chloe's, he handed over the dope.

My friend Hayden and I started doing coke together, too. I was so excited to have another friend who shared my love of the drug. We started making bogus excuses to leave work early so we could drive to Cabanas and get blow. I only bought from him a handful more times before he stopped selling—or at least that's what he told me. I think it might have had more to do with the fact I was not very secretive about my drug use or because I would blow his phone up with multiple text messages every night out.

If you've ever done cocaine, you know you can't simply stop doing cocaine. It controlled my entire state of mind. The second I had a drop of alcohol in my system, I immediately focused on obtaining coke. Work didn't matter anymore; drinking didn't matter anymore—all I wanted was to snort more powder.

Just because the only coke dealer I knew stopped selling didn't mean I was going to take no for an answer. I would walk around Cabana's literally asking anyone who would talk to me if they knew where I could find blow.

Reckless? Yes. Dangerous? Yes.

Effective? Most definitely.

These questions eventually led me to a short black guy named Sean. He definitely seemed more like a real drug dealer than I was used to, and I liked that about him. He was covered in tattoos and always carried a gun. I knew he wasn't the type to stop drug-dealing randomly, so he became my regular dealer. I would stop by his house on the way to work almost every night to pick up a small baggie of coke.

Being a white girl from a small town, it was a lot to get used to when going over to Sean's place. At any given time, he would have over three to five other black guys with guns who were always smoking weed and drinking codeine syrup. This is something that was impossible to witness in my hometown. I had never even met a black man in person until I moved to Florida. Sean had a recording room in his house, so he and his boys were always hanging out in their studio. It turned out that Sean was an aspiring rapper who sold coke to pay the bills—I'm sure I helped pay a number of them all by myself.

Hayden and I were inseparable together once we bonded over cocaine. We changed our work schedules so we only worked the same days. We would sneak into Infinity Island bathroom together to take shots of vodka or to snort whatever pill or powder we could get our hands on that day. We were absolutely crazy together. I actually had a whole Facebook photo album at one point of Hayden and I drinking straight out of a Crown Royale bottle while I drove. We stole the full bottle off someone else's table at a nightclub. Why I thought it was a good idea to post proof of me drinking and driving for the public to see, I have no idea. Besides the fact we both loved to be reckless, we were both broken girls who were overly hyper and needed heaps of attention. Although the majority of our memories together were doing something illegal, we were always laughing and having a good time.

At some point, Hayden and I morphed into almost identical versions of each other. We both dyed our hair black with purple bangs, we both had the exact same three facial piercing, and we would always coordinate our stripping and partying outfits to match each other. We both were on the same page in our lives and that page was living without regrets.

The thought that we had a drug problem never crossed my mind. We were young and having fun—wasn't that what every twenty-year-old did? We had a special tradition at every sleepover called "bumps in bed." In the morning when we would wake up together, we would chant the phrase over and over laughing as we did lines of coke before we even had our morning pee.

Hayden was a good distraction from Ryan, who I was still sleeping with on a regular basis. I wouldn't hang out with him, in fact, I have never hung out with that man sober once in our two-year on-again, off-again "relationship." I had zero self-control when I was fucked up at Cabanas, and I would give in to having sex with him in his Tahoe.

As I sit here writing this with actual respect for myself, I can't wrap my head around how I could dare sleep with the man who pretty much forced me to have an abortion. Maybe I stopped caring about myself and my well-being after that abortion. I let him manipulate and mind-fuck me so many times. I don't know why I couldn't cut him off completely, but he stayed in my life until I moved away from Pensacola.

It was around Christmastime when Hayden and I met our new partner in crime. Her name was Lauren and she was a few years older than us, which meant we finally could buy booze instead of stealing it. She was tall with dirty blonde hair, tattoos, and big natural boobs. Her "don't give a fuck" attitude intrigued me. She lived in an apartment with her younger brother (who I later learned was not her brother, just a close friend that she moved from her hometown to live with her).

Lauren was a good addition to our team because she too had no real responsibilities and could spend most nights in a blacked-out daze with us. We started spending a lot of time at Lauren's place and eventually Hayden moved into her spare room. With Lauren and Hayden under the same roof, I knew all I had to do was come over and there would be someone who was willing to party with me.

Lauren's younger "brother," Tyler, was only eighteen years old. This made it hard for us to all go out together. Sure, Hayden and I were underage, but because we had vaginas, we were always let inside the club. Not a lot of places wanted to be liable for letting an eighteen-year-old boy in. We spent the beginning of each night out finding ways to sneak Tyler into the clubs and bars, and it worked most of the time.

All four of us loved cocaine. We were visiting Sean around twice a night to buy from him. As much fun as Lauren, Hayden, Tyler, and I were having together—it would be short-lived. There is a time limit of how long four drug addicts can be under one roof together before they start to fight. That time limit is somewhere around five or six weeks. Hayden and Lauren were taking psychedelics and losing their minds. Lauren and I had a small crush on each other and hooked up often. On the other hand, something was beginning to develop between Tyler and me as well.

Tyler wasn't the kind of guy I would typically go for. He was a skinny blond boy who was years younger than me. We didn't have much in common besides the fact we loved cocaine, but there was an instant bond and we knew we always had each other's backs. Even though Tyler knew I was still regularly fucking Ryan, he pursued me. I would come back from the club crying about what awful thing Ryan said to me that night, and Tyler would give me lines of coke and tell me I deserved better while cuddling me to sleep.

It became obvious to Hayden and Lauren that there was something going on between Tyler and me, but it was more puppy love at that point. I never expected us to get into a relationship, but I did really like the guy. It was a refreshing change from Ryan's mental abuse.

Tyler gave me back rubs and advice and lines of cocaine, and he even gave me a cute nickname. He started calling me

"Boots," and soon Hayden and Lauren were calling me Boots as well. The nickname came from the fact I wore the same knee-high black boots literally every single day. Also, it was sort of poking fun at me for the way I pronounced the word with my Yooper accent. It was the first time I had a nickname, so it made me feel special.

Even though Tyler seemed like the sweetest guy, I was still stuck under Ryan's spell. You would think when someone genuine came along I would jump at the opportunity to treat them right, but there was something that kept me running back to Ryan.

One night I was hanging out with Tyler separate from Lauren and Hayden. We were in the back of a friend's truck waiting to buy drugs outside of Infinity Island. When we got out of the car and walked over to the guy, he came up on Tyler and punched him straight in the face, knocking him out.

"That's for Ryan" was the only thing the guy said before getting back into his car and taking off. I couldn't believe how quick it all happened, but when Tyler came to, it was clear he needed to go to the hospital. We pulled up at the emergency room, and before we went inside Tyler insisted we do a few bumps because who knew when we would be able to do them again or how long he'd be stuck in the hospital?

We walked into the emergency room and they immediately took Tyler back to a room. They told me I had to wait in the waiting room until he got settled and had a few tests done. I sat in the waiting room and Ryan started texting me asking me where I was so we could hang out (have sex). I was bored and drunk so I started replying and the next thing I knew I was telling Ryan he could come get me.

As I waited for Ryan to pick me up, all I could think about was what an asshole I would be if I really left Tyler alone at the hospital. I was his only support system and he was planning on seeing me any minute.

I ultimately chose going to sleep at Ryan's over being a good friend to Tyler (or more than friends, whatever we were at that point). I got into Ryan's car and he laughed about what had happened to Tyler, saying he deserved it. I felt so bad for leaving and for what had happened but clearly not bad enough.

The next day I texted Tyler with no reply, so I decided to text Lauren instead to see if she heard from Tyler. They were both very pissed off at me. Lauren had run to Tyler's side when she heard what had happened. She told me his jaw was broken and had to be wired shut for the next couple of months. I felt terrible that he essentially had a broken jaw because he was interested in dating me. I felt even worse for leaving his side after the whole assault happened. I went back to the hospital later that day to apologize and for some reason, he forgave me. When he was free to leave the hospital, I drove us back to Lauren's apartment.

But I could tell that we four friends were growing apart. Lauren kicked Hayden out after a drug-induced fight one night and soon after essentially kicked Tyler out too. I don't know whether Lauren liked me and didn't want Tyler to have me or if she liked Tyler and didn't want me to have him—either way, she was done with us fooling around with each other. She told Tyler he had to choose between me and her.

When Lauren kicked Hayden out of her apartment, Lauren decided to move out of the apartment as well. She had a sugar daddy a few miles away, some old rich guy who owned a condo on the beach, and he offered to let Lauren and Tyler live at his beach house for free.

Well, in exchange with sleeping with him.

Naturally, I pretty much lived there too since we were all inseparable. We didn't sleep in a room in the house; instead, we all stayed in the sugar daddy's garage he never used. We laid down two mattresses and set up a TV—that was all we needed. We were way too fucked up on drugs to care that we were living in a stranger's garage.

Once our group went from four to three, Lauren felt like the third wheel. I guess it doesn't take too long to get tired of two people having sex on the mattress directly next to yours every night. Not even a week into living in the garage, she told us I was no longer allowed to hang out with them. I wasn't allowed at the beach house, and she didn't want Tyler to even speak to me anymore.

"You either stop hanging out with Boots or you're not allowed here anymore either," she told him.

She was shocked that he chose me over her, and I was just as surprised. He had known Lauren for almost ten years and had only known me for two months. I felt honored that I was so important to someone, but also a bit scared for what was going to happen next.

I wasn't sure how we were going to make things work. I didn't have my own place and neither did Tyler. The only place I had to stay other than Lauren's sugar daddy's garage was my mom's house. Tyler's parents lived in Indiana, so he had nowhere else to go other than wherever I went. I knew there was little to no chance that my mom would go for letting Tyler live in her house.

I wasn't sure if I still had a job at Infinity Island because I was always out partying instead, and Tyler didn't have a job whatsoever. We definitely didn't have the money to get our own place together. We weren't even officially dating yet and already were faced with countless challenges.

The solution we came up with was something I never thought I would be a part of—and I owed it all to cocaine.

Drug Dealer Girlfriend

IT WAS THE BEGINNING of February when Tyler and I became boyfriend and girlfriend. It was also the same day we were packing all of his belongings because he was getting kicked out of the garage. The only assets he had in Florida were a backpack full of clothes and a couple snapbacks. He quickly packed his things and got into my car.

The night before Lauren kicked Tyler and me out of her sugar daddy's house, we watched a movie called *Belly*. It was a movie all about a life of crime, mainly drug dealing and robbery. Tyler and I took turns doing lines while watching the movie. We admired the guys in the movies and almost envied them for getting to live such a life.

"I should start selling dope," Tyler told me after doing a fat line of cocaine.

I knew he was serious because the kid didn't have a scared bone in his body. He might be a small, eighteen-year-old boy, but Tyler saw himself as a seven-foot thug. Nothing was too dangerous for him. Plus, he had already robbed a guy I used to sleep with, so I knew he was probably up to it.

When Tyler told me he was going to rob a man who I will leave unnamed, I didn't think he was really going to go through with it. I had jokingly told him how easy this guy would be to steal from because I knew where he kept his money and drugs, but I didn't think Tyler'd actually do it. I always assumed it was just the drugs talking, when he talking about hitting licks—the street term for robbing somebody. When Tyler called me up one day to ask exactly where this man's money and weed was hidden, I told him. He also asked the best way to break in. I let him know that the back door was perfect because it was barely ever locked and even if it was, the door would not be hard to break into.

I was working my shift at Infinity Island when he called back a couple hours later, detailing everything he had stolen from the guy's house. I couldn't believe he actually went through with it. I was slightly freaked out, but also slightly turned on by the bad boy persona he was forming. Tyler made decent money pawning all of the electronics, and we used the cash he stole to buy cocaine so we could celebrate him hitting his first lick in Pensacola. That is, if you didn't count him stealing Lauren's sugar daddy's wallet out of his pocket during his nap—but that was kind of an amateur move compared to what he had just done. Along with the other items he stole was a huge amount of weed. We weren't sure what to do with it. Neither of us were stoners; we just loved tweaking off of cocaine.

After officially leaving Lauren's with no chance of return-ing, Tyler and I started talking about what we were going to do to survive. We needed a place to stay, and we needed money.

That's when Tyler brought up the movie we had watched the night before. He wanted to start a new career as a drug dealer. He was absolutely crazy. And I was just as crazy to agree to be his partner in crime—literally.

We went straight to Sean's and showed him the giant stash of marijuana he had stolen and offered to give it all to Sean to sell for profit. The catch? He wanted Sean to put him on the drug game.

Tyler was not the type of guy you thought of when you pictured your average drug dealer, so Sean was reasonably wary of his ability to sell dope. However, because of all the weed he had given him for practically nothing, he agreed to front him a gram of cocaine to see what he could do with it.

If you have any experience with legitimate drug dealers, then you know it's basically impossible for a dealer to agree to give you a front. A front is when you don't have to pay for the drugs when you get them, only when you earn the money to pay them back. We may have just stepped in the world of drug dealing, but we both knew we were lucky to get fronted blow. We weren't going to fuck this up.

We left Sean's house with a gram of blow to sell and headed back to my mom's house. She and my stepdad were used to me showing up whenever I felt like it. I could be gone a month and my mom wouldn't even care to check up on how I was doing, so I hoped she would be just as laid-back about my new boyfriend coming into her house. I briefly introduced him before we went into my bedroom.

She seemed fine with him being there, so I hoped she would be fine with him living there for a while as well. We didn't really have any other options. I explained the situation to my mom and though she wasn't happy, she said he could stay for a few days until we figured out a permanent solution.

Locked inside my room together, Tyler and I stared at the baggie of coke. Do you know how hard it is for two coke addicts not to snort the cocaine in their possession? But this was business and Tyler had to prove that he could be a part of the dope game.

To make a profit off of cocaine, you have two options. You can either sell it for higher than you bought it for, or you can cut it.

Cutting coke consisted of mixing in other white powders to make it look like more coke than it actually was. A lot of people cut their cocaine with baking soda but we had a much better solution. We would go to every gas station to buy all of the NoDoz we could get our hands on. We would take the white tablets and crush them down to a fine powder. Mixing cocaine with the NoDoz was a genius way to cut the drug because instead of baking soda, which does not have an effect on you, the NoDoz will make you jittery and energetic, much like coke would. This way, we could easily turn one gram into two. So if we bought a gram for $60 we would make $120 off of it.

What would we do with that $60 of profit?

Spend it on a gram of coke for ourselves, of course.

If Tyler and I weren't addicts ourselves, we could've surely made enough money to get our own apartment and live like normal human beings. Instead, we decided we were only going to be drug dealers so we could do free coke. I must say, while being a cocaine addict, nothing is better than being able to do grams of cocaine for free every day.

Tyler brought Sean the sixty dollars for the gram he fronted him later that night. Sean was taken aback by how fast Tyler could flip product, and in return he fronted Tyler a ball. A ball of cocaine is three and a half grams, and this is when you can start to make a good amount of money if you're committed. Which we were—but we were also in love with the drug. We both did a few key bumps on the way home to cut the ball. Tyler told me we could turn it into six or seven grams of coke, so there was no reason we couldn't do a little of it ourselves before we mixed it with NoDoz.

We started off responsibly, only doing a little of the cocaine we were supposed to be selling before we cut it. All we had to do was sell all of the coke and our free coke would be waiting for us at the end. It was motivation to sell quickly.

Tyler brought back the money for the front on the ball the next day and from then on Sean had no problem trusting him. Tyler would even make drug runs for Sean, until one day Sean stopped answering his phone. We decided to stop by and see what was going on, and instead of Sean answering the door like normal, a five-foot-tall, angry white woman answered the door. I recognized her as always being in the background when we would come over to buy coke. It was his girlfriend, Destiny.

She informed us that Sean had been arrested and that she would be taking over his drug-dealing business. I never heard Destiny talk much when Sean was around, but now that she was on her own, she had quite the attitude. She was not someone whose bad side you would want to be on. Like Sean, she carried a pistol and didn't take shit from anyone.

Destiny wasn't as fond of the idea of fronting Tyler drugs as Sean had been, but she was fond of the fact that there were two drug addicts over everyday who would pretty much do anything for some coke. I was always dropping Tyler off at Destiny's to help her go sell. I'd do my own thing while they drove around dealing all day, then I'd meet them back at her house when they were done. We'd spend hours sitting on Destiny's floor snorting lines off of her framed *Scarface* photo with all of the money Tyler made that day.

Through the entirety of our relationship, Tyler and I probably averaged a ball of coke combined each day. Sometimes more, sometimes less. It became a regular routine of taking care of one another when we got so high that we would turn blue. It happened to Tyler first and I had no idea what to do. His hands and feet turned blue and he was simply not there. He dazed off into space, not reacting to me slapping him or yelling at him to see if he was okay. He was shaking and ice cold.

I ran a hot tub and made him get in. We were at my mom's house, and it was maybe five in the morning. I grabbed crackers from the pantry and forced him to eat a couple. Both of us would barely eat because we were spending all our money on drugs and were too high to have an appetite.

We would both bring the life back into each other multiple times in the coming months.

Our daily schedule consisted of waking up in the afternoon and starting our day with some lines. We were so obsessed that we would set up the lines before we went to sleep to make sure we could do coke immediately upon waking up. If I was too tired to wake up when Tyler had people he needed to go sell to, he would roll up a dollar bill, fill it with coke, then pour it down my nose while I was sleeping. Nothing wakes you up quicker than cocaine.

Under my bed is where we always hid my pink Juicy Couture box that we put all of our drugs and cutting supplies in. We probably did over a hundred grams of blow off the top of that box. For Valentine's Day, Tyler's "present" to me was a giant heart-shaped line off the top of the box.

After waking up and doing some blow, we would get ready for the day and go drive around for hours selling coke to all of our clients. Since Tyler didn't have a car or even a license, we were always together when the deals would go down. When we needed money, we wouldn't just wait for people to call us—we would call them. Whether we had to tell them we had a great deal for them or some fire new coke, we lied our asses off to make money so we could do more drugs.

After driving around all afternoon, we would head to Cabanas or Destiny's to do more drugs and to try to sell more drugs. Our nightly drug binges lasted until the sun came up and/or until we were completely out of money. We repeated this pattern each and every day.

My mom told me Tyler had to find another place to live and I explained we didn't have money to go anywhere else. I couldn't just drop him off on a street somewhere and tell him to figure it out. We were a team, and if he wasn't going to be allowed to stay there, then I wasn't going to stay there. Just like he gave up his free place at Lauren's for me, I gave up my free place at my mom's for him.

With no place to sleep, Tyler thought Destiny would have our backs and let us stay with her since we were helping her out so much. When we weren't helping her sell drugs, we were giving her our money to buy drugs. Why wouldn't she want two cokeheads living in her living room constantly giving her money for more blow? She said we only could stay for a couple days, but we took it. We decided we would figure out where to go next when the time came. And so this is what we did for the next two months. Whenever we got kicked out of one place, we moved on to the next person who would let us crash.

Destiny's house wasn't ideal for anyone to live in. She lived in a tiny, run-down house in the hood. The type of neighborhood where you could get shot just for looking at someone wrong while driving down the street. She had the worst of criminals in and out of her house at all hours of the day. At the time, we liked the danger of the hood. We called her place The Trap House—the trap is where people sell drugs and trapping was what you called selling drugs.

Since Destiny was doing this favor for us, she wanted us to help her with a favor as well. Sean was still in jail but working for the inmate work camp. He told Destiny where to go and where to hide drugs for him. We drove to the work camp around midnight one night. There wasn't much around the area and there was no one to witness the crime we were about to commit.

Destiny had a cigarette box filled with weed and we were told to hop the fence and to hide it behind the big tree. I can't imagine the consequences we would've gotten ourselves into if we got caught, but somehow we always had good luck when it came to committing crimes.

After stashing the drugs for Sean, we ran and jumped the fence, fueled by the biggest adrenaline rush of our lives—which is saying a lot for cocaine addicts.

As convenient as it was for Destiny to have two minions willing to do whatever she asked living with her, she got tired of it quickly. We would be sleeping on her couch until dinnertime when she was having customers over to buy drugs, and we were kicked out a couple days later.

Tyler had a plan for who we could mooch off of next. There was an old guy named William that we sold to once. He was at least in his mid-fifties, and the only reason we knew of him was because he was our friend Jennifer's sugar daddy.

Jennifer was my age and had long blonde hair and a nice body. It grossed me out thinking she slept with such an old man—but it was her business, not mine. William had small parties every once in a while when Jennifer would ask him to.

The parties consisted of maybe ten kids our age with booze and coke supplied by William. Not a bad deal.

We had only met William twice in our lives before we decided to stop by his house unannounced. The first time was when Jennifer invited us to his place to drink. That's when we discovered William liked cocaine, and Tyler jumped on that opportunity. He told William he knew someone who could get him a ball, and William was stoked that Tyler had a hookup for him.

Of course, he didn't trust us to drive alone with his money and come back with the drugs. William said he would drive Tyler over to Sean's to make the deal for him. I stayed at the party with Jennifer, anxiously awaiting putting cocaine up my nose.

When they came back from Sean's house, I was relieved I would finally be able to get high.

William went to take the ball out of his pocket when a look of panic came over his face.

"Where the hell is my coke?"

How does someone lose two hundred dollars' worth of drugs in a car ride home? Tyler, Jennifer, and William all ran outside to retrace their steps. They checked the stairs, the driveway, and the car. When they came back ten minutes later, I could see everyone was disappointed.

"It must've fallen out of my pocket as we were walking out of Sean's." It was the only logical explanation that William could come up with, so he had Jennifer drive back over to Sean's with him to look further. We were all itching to get our fix, especially me and Tyler. We were used to steadily doing bumps of cocaine all throughout the day but it had been at least ten hours since we had any. I was furious that someone could misplace their cocaine. That shit was precious!

Once William was gone, Tyler gave me a look and my whole face lit up. I knew that little thief had the coke. We went to the bathroom together and Tyler showed me he had pocketed the drugs. When he was searching in the car with the others for the drugs, he had spotted it and quickly put it in his pocket and continued to search.

I couldn't have been happier that William was such an idiot to let it get out of his possession. If Tyler was around, he would find a way to steal anything anyone left out of their sight. Tyler and I left the party and drove around the rest of that night doing line after line.

The second time we met William was at another party at his house. We were still high after selling coke all night and wanted to keep going. Jennifer was at Cabanas with us, so we convinced her to tell William that we should all after-party there. I'm sure the poor old man was already asleep at that time, but with his twenty-year-old hot sugar baby coming over, was he really going to say no? I couldn't believe anyone would sleep with William for money, and in my head there wasn't enough money (or drugs) in the world to make me sleep with someone so old and unattractive.

This time we wanted to make money off of William. We had our own (shitty) coke that we were trying to get rid of that we convinced him to buy. He bought two grams and we made $120 off of $60 of coke. Even though we knew half of the powder was NoDoz, we still snorted it with William and Jennifer. That's the thing about being an addict: you're desperate. We were just happy that we were basically getting paid to do free cocaine.

By the end of that night, we were all drunk and tweaking off of the powder. Jennifer and William went into his room and locked the door. This left Tyler and me with the baggie of coke alone. We took it and finished it on the way home that night.

I wasn't sure how William was going to react to us showing up at his house. If he had one ounce of common sense he would realize we were thieves who were always stealing his drugs. Thank god William didn't have common sense.

We walked into his house without even knocking to find him and his thirteen-year-old son watching a football game. Tyler told me the plan would be to act as natural as possible. No knocking, no explaining why we just randomly showed up, and to act like it was our own place. I went along with the plan. William seemed surprised to see us but not mad like a normal person would be when two young drug addicts walk into their house without warning.

Letting Tyler handle the talking, I went to his spare bedroom to do a few lines. I felt very uncomfortable asking people to let us live with them, especially an old man who had a son. I knew he wouldn't tell us we could live there, so I kept nervously snorting drugs until Tyler came into the room to tell me the outcome.

"Well? What did he say?"

The anticipation was killing me.

"I didn't ask. We will just play it cool and act like it's fine for us to stay here."

I couldn't believe that Tyler didn't even ask William if we were allowed over. Instead we just made ourselves at home. All the spare bedroom had was an air-mattress with a disgusting comforter on top and a plastic table with a chair. That was our home for the next month or so. I could not, and still cannot, wrap my head around what the heck William was thinking, but he never once questioned our presence in his home.

We would sleep all day long in that room and when we woke up, we would leave. After driving around trapping all night, we would return to William's house to crash. Sometimes when we would leave for the night, William would be sitting in his living room with one of his friends or even his son. We would just say "see you later" and walk out of his place.

It felt so awkward and wrong that no one was even acknowledging the situation, but at that point we had to take what we could get. This went on for about three weeks until one day William stopped us when we were about to leave his house.

"I'm going out of the country next week so you're going to have to find somewhere else to stay. I'm going to be gone for a few weeks."

We told him that was fine and that we would find somewhere to go when the time came. I was tired of tiptoeing around the spare bedroom whenever I was awake anyways. I didn't even want to flush the toilet to make any noise, because it would remind William that we were living off of him. I was terrified to be kicked out and forced to live in my car.

We spent most of the time in my car anyways. While we rode around—me always driving, Tyler sitting in the passenger's seat—we would constantly be doing key bumps. He would give them to me as I was driving, blasting rap music. We had a playlist of about ten songs that we would listen to over and over again. All of the songs had to do with selling drugs and living life in the hood, something we took pride in.

Although we were struggling with finding a place to live, we were having the time of our lives. We got to do free cocaine everyday by forcing the same group of people to buy our coke regularly. We had the Bonnie-and-Clyde type of relationship that every thug yearns for. We were now known around the hood as Jit and Boots—Jit or "juvenile in training" was a term for a young thug, and the nickname fit Tyler perfectly. People only called me Boots because that's how he always introduced me.

William's departure was around the time things started to spiral out of control. One night we got to William's house in the middle of the night so we could go to sleep, but his door was locked. He must have been leaving the next morning and wanted to make sure we weren't still sleeping in his spare bedroom when he left town.

With nowhere else to go, we spent the night sleeping in my car and plotting for the next morning. We were certain that we knew how to solve all of our problems—at least for the time being. The solution? We would break into William's house and live there while he was away. He wouldn't have to know, and we wouldn't have to be homeless.

The heat woke us up early the next afternoon. Florida is probably the worst state for living out of your vehicle. We did a few lines off of the center console and it was time to put our plan into action.

We pulled up to his house and the front door was locked, as we figured. We went around the back of his house and went up the stairs onto his back porch balcony. The doors were locked in the back too, but we weren't going to give up. There was one other set of doors along his porch that was never used. We actually had never even noticed them before. Tyler turned the door handle and it wasn't locked, but for some reason the door would not budge open. We pressed our faces against the glass to see his couch on the other side of the door. Well, no wonder no one used that door: the couch was blocking it. From the inside it just looked like two big windows. With the weight of both of us pushing against the door together, we managed to move the couch enough so we could climb into his house.

Once inside, we made sure no one else was home and then celebrated by doing more coke. We now had a solid place to stay for a few weeks and for the first time ever, a place all to ourselves. We drank his liquor and blasted music all night long while cutting up cocaine.

Tyler learned a foolproof trick to make our customers think we had the purest coke. It was called "rerocking." After we would cut the shit out of the coke with NoDoz, we would take a few drops of water on our fingers and sprinkle it lightly into the baggie. Then we would tie the bag, put it on the ground, and stomp on it a few times. We'd have to put it in the freezer for a few minutes without touching it to make sure it hardened. Once it was dry, it would lightly break apart and form rock-like shapes. If you were educated on cocaine then you knew to always looked for rocks, which usually meant the cocaine was pure and "straight off the brick." Unless you were buying from me and Tyler—then it was just rerocked.

With the privacy of having our "own" place and not having to drive around all day to occupy our time until we made sales, we started wanting to do more cocaine. Instead of just taking a gram for ourselves out of the eight balls we were going to be selling, we started doing half of it all. We would be up, tweaked out of our minds, craving more of the powder. Even though we already cut the rest of the coke into a disgusting amount of NoDoz, we would keep taking more for ourselves as the night grew longer. Pretty soon we would only have a gram left when we were supposed to have three and a half grams of (cut) coke to sell. Our drug use got so severe that sometimes we were left to sell crushed-up NoDoz and pass it off as cocaine because we had snorted all of our product.

There was no controlling us anymore. We weren't making enough money because we were snorting all the coke instead of selling it. Usually we would re-up with a ball to cut and sell, but now we could barely afford a gram.

Tyler wouldn't allow me to strip, and I missed Infinity Island dearly. The cocaine and our relationship were more important to me than my job, though. Even when we were having money issues, he still said I wasn't allowed to work. I'd be damned if I ever let a man tell me what to do nowadays, but back then I was naïve and weak. I suggested one of the websites I used to go on back in my web-camming days as a perfect way to make us extra money. With this one, I didn't even have to get on camera. The guys on the site literally had to pay to talk to the girls, and each message would cost them a dollar to reply to.

The site became our new obsession. Tyler would sit on there for hours upon hours, messaging the men, pretending to be me. We needed something to do while we were high as hell off of the coke anyway. We started making up to a hundred dollars a night by dirty-talking on the Internet, which meant more drugs for us.

Our success as drug dealers was quickly fading, however, and even Destiny wouldn't give us cocaine anymore. She was annoyed at how often we were bothering her and refused to ever front us. That's when Tyler ran across a new drug dealer.

BT was a big, tall black guy who proudly wore his weapon in plain sight for us to see when he came over to talk business. Tyler convinced him to front us a ball, promising that we would pay him back the next day. The problem was that we did the entire ball that night and had zero dollars to give him in return. We couldn't make any money by selling because we had nothing left to sell.

We could make money online but it would still take three business days until the money transferred to my bank account.

We were screwed. BT called Tyler's phone repeatedly, and when we saw "1 New Voicemail" pop up on his phone screen, our stomachs turned.

"Jit, you better not be tryin' to avoid me. I need my money. I better not hear any excuses. I know where you stay."

It was clear we had no choice but to come up with the money—and fast. As much as I missed Infinity Island, dancing to make the money was out of the question. Tyler forbade me from stripping, something I resented him for. I moved to Florida for the sole purpose of being a stripper, and his jealousy was out of control. Tyler would talk down to me for being a stripper and said he would leave me if I did it again.

I started to rethink our relationship. I was tired of being controlled and tired of not having a home. Tyler would even tell me what clothes I could or couldn't wear. I missed hanging out with my friends that he'd forbid to me see. But, man, the "free" drugs were amazing.

With stripping and selling drugs out of the question, we only had one way left that we knew how to make money: robbery. Sitting in William's place with no drugs or money, we felt defeated. We kept trying to come up with people we knew to rob when Tyler realized we were already inside someone else's house. We went into William's son's room and Tyler put his Xbox in his backpack.

I felt bad stealing from a young boy, but I also didn't want to be shot by BT. We thought about going to a pawnshop, but Tyler had a better idea. Although the pawnshop could give us cash, it would be retraceable if William went to the cops. He let Destiny know that we hit a lick and he had some electronics that he could trade her for some drugs. An hour later, Destiny handed us over a ball for the Xbox and Tyler's laptop.

We now had to get rid of the coke—and quick—before BT tracked us down. I drove around all day while Tyler ran into the workplaces and houses of our regulars, begging them to buy. I don't know about you, but if my coke dealer showed up unannounced asking me to buy, I'd be sketched out and stop dealing with them, which happened with one client. But the rest agreed. By the end of the night we had BT's money.

Even though he knew we had his money, I was still nervous around BT. I didn't know if he was going to be angry that we ignored his phone calls the entire day. I told Tyler I didn't want to be involved in the money handoff. The last thing I wanted was for him to jump in my back seat and shoot me in the head.

We drove to the mall, one of our regular spots to go when we had nothing else to do during the day. We spent many sleep-deprived mornings at the Cordova Mall, going in and out of the family restroom—the perfect restroom for cocaine-addicted couples. Both male and female could go inside and they had a huge sink counter that we could cut lines on. We gave no thought to the families with children who might *actually* need to be using that restroom. Then again, what drug addict isn't selfish?

It's embarrassing to think how cracked out we would be in that bathroom. I can remember a handful of times where we would think we must've dropped some coke on the floor below the sink. We would search the black floor mat for white specks and collect them to put back on top of the counter. It is safe to say 100 percent of those white specks were not cocaine, but in our addicted minds, we had to take the chance just in case we were wasting any blow. So we'd collect a pile of bathroom floor germs and snort that pile too.

I waited inside the mall while Tyler ran out to BT's car to give him the money. I remember being so petrified for him. It was a real possibility that Tyler would not return. BT was a real gangster and did not play around. We made him wait an extra twenty-four hours for his money, so I wasn't expecting him to be thrilled to see Tyler—even if he was handing over a wad of cash.

I finally breathed again when I saw Tyler walking back into the mall unharmed five minutes later. We were both exhausted. We had been running around on no sleep in a drug-induced haze the last two days trying to get BT's money. We headed back to William's to get some sleep, even though it was noon.

Our happiness was starting to fade. We were right back at square one with no money or drugs. Reality started to hit—there was only so long we could go on living this way together.

It had been over two months of daily cocaine usage. I'm talking full-on, morning-to-night, unable-to-function-without-it usage. If we didn't have cocaine, I would refuse to get out of bed. I would feel sick like I was really going to die, but the second Tyler would return with some dope, I would be my normal self again. If we ran out of cocaine in the middle of the day—or night—we would both be in a silent panic, trying to figure out who to sell complete crap to or who to steal from.

Along with the constant drug use came starvation. The use of hard drugs and a lack of an appetite go hand in hand. Because we were using drugs throughout the day, we were never hungry. It was only when we were absolutely defeated or completely out of cocaine that we would realize we hadn't eaten in days.

Of course, when we would be sober enough to grasp the fact that we needed food, we were out of money. We could usually find enough change to go get ramen noodle cups from the gas station. Sometimes Tyler would even steal candy for me by shoving it down his pants. But 90 percent of what we ate was definitely ramen; the other 10 percent was McDonald's chicken nuggets. Around that time, they had a really cheap deal on a box of twenty nuggets. Being able to afford McDonald's was a luxury compared to the twenty-eight-cent ramen noodle cups we normally ate.

As you can imagine, surviving on only drugs without food or sleep can turn even the most stable person downright crazy. The worst it ever got was when we were convinced William's house had been bugged by the police. We just knew that they were on to us for breaking and entering and that they must've wired his house while we were out. They wanted to catch us talking about robbing and drug dealing. That's when we decided it was too risky to carry on a conversation out loud with each other. We spent the entire day in silence, typing back and forth to each other on a blank computer document. Terrified we were going to wind up in prison, we kept peering out the blinds expecting a whole squad of cop cars to bust us any minute. Of course, this was all in our heads.

In our minds, everyone was after us. Every car was following us, every cop car knew we were drug dealers, every person in the bar was planning on trying to steal our coke. Tyler and I even started getting paranoid that we were stealing drugs from each other. He started hiding the bags of drugs from me and I started to fight with him, claiming that I knew he wasn't sharing.

Living in this constant state of mind while dealing with getting BT his money, we were ready for a good night (day) of sleep. We got back to William's empty house and we were in for a surprise. The power was out. We were afraid William got word of us living in his house but hoped maybe he just had the power turned off to save money on bills.

We tried his power box to see if there was just a switch turned off, but that wasn't the case. Then we went outside to the power line next to his house and found a box, but we couldn't get it open. Turns out the real reason the power was off was because William's ex-wife had drained his bank accounts and therefore his bills weren't getting paid.

That poor man—everyone in his life was using him.

Living without electricity is extremely difficult. However, if you sleep the entire day and stay awake all night, it is nearly impossible. We would have to cut our coke and do lines only using the light of a lighter. After a couple of days, we knew this wasn't a life we could continue living much longer. Our lives were falling apart.

It was the beginning of May when we woke up to yelling in the next room.

"WHAT THE FUCK! WHAT THE FUCK IS GOING ON?!"

William had just returned from vacation to see his big screen TV missing— another possession of his we had sold for coke. Tyler and I thought we still had at least a week before he would return home. We were in his guest bedroom and it was only a matter of time before he would bust in the room to see if we were there. Part of me wanted us to take the chance he wouldn't check the guest room and just hide in there until he went to sleep, but something told me that he wasn't going to bed anytime soon.

Tyler somehow had the balls to leave the bedroom to go confront William. I stayed in the dark bedroom, silently having a panic attack. I wanted cocaine to try to calm myself down, but we had nothing.

I thought Tyler was going to defuse the situation, but William's screaming had hit an all-time high. I pressed my ear against the door to eavesdrop on the conversation. Tyler was yelling for him to put his gun down, and that's when I came to the conclusion that we were about to die. William was going to kill us, and maybe we deserved it.

I could hear a scuffle in the next room, and I hid inside of the closet hoping he wouldn't know I was in his house, too.

Ten or fifteen minutes had passed when I heard things quiet down. When things got silent was when I started worrying the most. Was Tyler dead? I didn't hear a gunshot, but I couldn't figure out what was going on.

KARMEN AMBER VAN DE BUNT

Hearing the door open to that bedroom, I thought my life was seconds from being over. "Boots?"

It was Tyler entering the bedroom. I jumped out of the closet in tears, asking what the hell had happened. William had had Tyler backed against a wall with his shotgun, threatening him. Tyler told him that we'd stopped by to see if he was back in town and found the door unlocked. That we came inside to see the TV was missing and knew something was wrong, so we stayed over until he got back so we could watch the house for him. I'm not sure how or if William believed this story.

The way Tyler got him to calm down was to tell him to call the cops and that he would tell them what he knew. This made him seem more reputable, but I still didn't think it was believable. I didn't want anything to do with the police so I stayed out of it while Tyler put on a good show for the officer that came by. They said they would dust for fingerprints and investigate further. I'm not sure what came of the situation, because that was the last night we ever spoke to William.

We calmly left the house at the same time the cop was leaving and got into my car. Once we drove away, handcuff-free, we freaked out. We were so close to being caught and we both had no idea how we hadn't been instantly arrested.

With nowhere left to go, we headed to my mom's house—though it was already crystal clear that Tyler was not allowed over anymore. Along with not wanting my boyfriend living off of them for free, my mom and stepdad also discovered my little brother's money had gone missing. This is something Tyler denies doing to this day. Part of me wouldn't be surprised if my mom stole the money herself so that Tyler could take the blame.

On the way to my mom's, we decided to make a quick pit stop at Destiny's. We'd had two hundred dollars just hit the direct deposit from the money we made online, so naturally we took out all two hundred dollars and used it on cocaine.

We got to my mom's around ten o'clock that night and everyone was already in bed. I snuck Tyler into my bedroom and locked my door. We weren't there more than a few minutes before we started arguing. We both knew that we couldn't keep living like this. It was getting too risky and now that the cops had Tyler's name for the police report at William's house, we really couldn't keep taking chances. We also knew by sunrise that my mom would kick Tyler out of her house and that we would have no place to go.

The argument between us quickly turned physical. Tyler pushed me on his way to leave my bedroom and I grabbed onto him, not letting him walk away. We were as silent as we possibly could be since everyone in the house was sleeping. Only whispering rude remarks back and forth.

Tyler said he was leaving, and I didn't want him to walk out that door. I fought with all my might to hold him back, but he shoved me so hard that I lost my balance and fell to the floor. Just like that, he was gone. The worst part: he took the coke with him.

I sat in my room crying, not knowing where Tyler went or if he would even come back. I knew in my heart that it was over. He returned an hour later and pulled out the Juicy Couture box from underneath my bed. Without a word, he pulled out the ball of coke and emptied the entire contents onto the box. I watched in silence, not knowing where he was going with this. After finely chopping it all up, he divided the three and a half grams into two lines.

"Fuck it," he said. "If this is going to be our last time doing coke together then let's go big." Tyler snorted one of the entire lines in almost one snort. He handed the dollar bill over to me and told me to do the other line. This was no ordinary line—

it was almost a two-gram line. Usually it took us at least an hour to go through two grams *together*. It took me a few tries to get the whole line up my nose, and I have never been higher than in that moment.

We weren't sure if we were going to die from doing a massive amount of blow in only a few seconds, but I don't think we would have minded either way. It wouldn't have stopped us. Chain-smoking an entire pack and a half of cigarettes, we sat outside until the sun came up. We didn't talk much, but we both knew our time together was over.

We left the house before anyone woke up and drove into town. I didn't want Tyler to leave. It was May, and it was beginning to get too hot to sleep in our car all day. I proposed that we could find a cheap motel to live in. We made our rounds to several different motels and hotels, all with monthly prices we knew we couldn't pay. We tried to sleep in one of the hotel lobbies, but we were quickly kicked out as soon as we started nodding off.

We were having withdrawals and feeling like utter death. I broke down into tears, and for the first time ever, Tyler did too. He stood outside my car and called his mom. I knew there was nothing I could do to make him stay, so I just sat in my car bawling loudly. It was probably a combination of sleep deprivation and drug use, but his leaving felt like the end of the world.

His mom bought him a plane ticket for later that afternoon. We sat and cried. Tyler told me he would go home for a couple months until I made enough money for our own apartment. Of course, I wouldn't be selling drugs by myself, so he knew I would have to go back to stripping. I missed Infinity Island more than ever and was secretly excited to go back and get some freedom again. He didn't like the idea of me stripping but because I "needed" to make money for us to be together, he allowed it.

We parked at the airport and had sex one last time in the passenger seat of my car. He came inside of me, which left a cum stain on my black interior. I told myself I would never try to wash that stain out so I could remember our last moments together.

I had a collection of pink air freshener trees, probably over twenty of them, hanging from my rearview mirror. Tyler took each and every one of them and wrote cute love notes and positive messages on them for me to read while he was gone. He kept promising that we would be reunited as quickly as I could come up with apartment money and that we would still be together forever.

An hour before his flight, he told me it was time for him to go. I couldn't let him walk away and I couldn't control my emotions. After I finally mustered the courage to let go of him, he walked backward the entire way into the airport, waving goodbye. When he was out of sight, I got a text message from him.

"I walked backward so you know I'm not turning my back on you and our love."

That text made it impossible for me to drive home with all of the tears welling up in my eyes. At that moment I truly thought I would see Tyler again and that our love could survive the long distance.

I would feel differently soon.

Working at Infinity Island doing drugs was much different than working there without them. The night would fly by and I would spend the entire shift in and out of the bathroom. My focus was on cocaine and partying and less about making money.

I started to dread having to do private dances, something every stripper hopes to get, just because I was so preoccupied with doing coke. As soon as I had made sixty dollars that night,

I would call Destiny to come bring a gram by the strip club. This trend made leaving the club with any money by the end of the night nearly impossible. I spent almost every dirty dollar bill on drugs.

A few months went by and Tyler and I were still officially dating. Long distance was hard, but we would Skype each other every night. Even when I worked, he would wait up long enough to call or Skype me at the end of the night. I'm sure this was more to keep tabs on me than because he cared to talk. Not a day went by without an argument. Each argument was based on him thinking I was cheating, and I was.

Ryan and I were sleeping together on a regular basis again. He would occasionally take pictures of me while I was going down on him or when we were having sex, but I never cared. That was until Ryan decided to send a picture to Tyler.

I told Tyler that the picture was an old photo, back from when I was dating Ryan. The lie was pointless because I had hot pink hair in the photo. I had never dyed my hair pink until Tyler and I started dating. I was caught red-handed...or pink-haired.

I told him I was sorry and that I was blacked-out (not a lie), but of course that didn't make it any better. I was fully ready to accept him breaking up with me, but to my surprise, he didn't. What he did do was much worse. He called Destiny and told her to cut me off.

It didn't work, thank God. At the end of the day, Destiny wanted to make her money, not get involved in my relationship drama, but I was appalled that Tyler would try to keep me away from cocaine.

I'm not sure why I kept trying to make the relationship work and why I didn't just break up with him after he moved away. I guess I thought I really loved the kid. We did have a special bond, and sharing so many rock-bottom moments with someone really connects you, but we were not meant to be with each other.

Finally, on my twenty-first birthday, the inevitable happened. Tyler told me I wasn't allowed to drink on my birthday. I laughed. I had waited years to be able to legally drink at the bars and clubs around Pensacola, and I sure as hell wasn't going to stay sober for a rocky relationship.

I decided I would work at Infinity Island on August 4, the day before my actual birthday. That way, when the clock struck midnight, I could legally drink. I could go out after and party elsewhere. I told Tyler I was going to work at Infinity Island and that I was going to drink, and he was not happy. He blew up my phone all night trying to make sure I wasn't doing anything "bad." However, once midnight approached, I would no longer be responding to any of Tyler's calls or texts.

Infinity's DJ announced before midnight that I was about to turn twenty-one. Every customer in the strip club bought a shot to hand me once midnight came. It was my bright idea that I wanted to take twenty-one shots for my twenty-first birthday. I accomplished this within five minutes. I vaguely remember falling off of the stage into a customer's lap only a few minutes after midnight.

The next thing I remember is waking up in my bed the next morning with a hangover from hell and no idea how I had gotten home. I tried to find my phone, but it was nowhere to be found. I noticed my acrylic nails were broken. Not just one or two like a normal drunk night, but all ten nails were busted off. My pink extensions were in a matted ball on the floor and my car was not in my driveway. Something had clearly gone very wrong. I was used to waking up not remembering the night before, but never had I been so reckless that I didn't know where my car was.

 Amber van de Bunt

I scrambled through my bag, trying to find any clues from the night before. After charging my phone, I immediately posted a Facebook status:

"UMMMM does anyone know where my car is?? Just woke up at home but my car isn't here! WTF happened last night? Being 21 sucks."

About twenty minutes later, one of the strippers from my club commented on my status saying she drove me home last night. I had zero recollection of the entire night. She informed me that some of the girls had found me passed out on the toilet with my head hanging completely inside of the bathroom garbage next to me.

Disgusting.

She'd put me in her back seat and dropped me off at the end of the night. I was shocked. This stripper and I didn't talk much; plus, I always took her for being the type to steal an unconscious girl's money, and I woke up with money in my bag.

I was thankful.

When I finished puking up liters of stomach bile, I realized I had over fifty text messages from Tyler. I wasn't in the mood to deal with his yelling. I was barely clinging to life, but I called him back to explain what had happened anyways.

He screamed at me, saying he didn't believe me. He said that he knew I was out partying and cheating on him. The reality was that I had passed out just after midnight, but nothing I could say would change his mind. That's when he finally broke up with me. After all of the months of struggling to survive, let alone to get along—we were over. He was done.

Happy birthday to me.

Although part of me was happy the relationship was over, I was still hurt he chose to ruin my birthday by trying to control my every move the night before and by breaking up with me the day of. I told myself I would never be in another toxic relationship as long as I lived. I was tired of being controlled, talked down to, and manipulated. Three out of the four relationships I had been in at that point were with very controlling men.

My mom told me that for my birthday we could go get tattoos, and I knew exactly what I was going to get: "Know Your Worth" on the top of my shoulder. It was so I could have a daily reminder that I deserved more than what I had previously let myself settle for. Later on down the road, the Internet would have a field day making fun of me when porn box covers showed me with a dick in my mouth and my "Know Your Worth" tattoo. Say what you want, but to this day that tattoo means a lot to me. Mostly because my most toxic relationship was yet to come.

Now, I was single and legally allowed to drink.

Flirting with Death

AUGUST TO OCTOBER WAS a nonstop party. I was working at Infinity Island a few times a week and the rest of the days I was partying at Cabanas. I rarely spent even one night a week sober, and that only happened when I was too hungover to drink again. Usually the thought of doing more cocaine would be enough motivation to get me out of bed, though. I would cure each day's hangover with more booze, something that was working very successfully.

A girl I had hung out with occasionally and had a lot in common with soon became my inseparable best friend. Her name was Jasmine, and she was gorgeous. She had tattoos and piercings and colorful hair like me. We were even the same height and the same weight.

We looked so similar that people often got us confused with one another. We were two peas in a pod, always on the same page. We both stripped at Infinity Island and loved booze and cocaine. We were the perfect friends for each other. Although we were nearly identical in every way, Jasmine could definitely handle herself much better than I could. A normal night out included us pregaming, stripping, going to the bars, having sex with each other in her bed, and passing out.

This was always followed the next morning by Jasmine having to tell me what happened the night before, because I would black out every night. I was always amazed that she could recall the details of what we had done when I couldn't remember a thing. Blacking out was now a normal occurrence, and I would even find it funny that I couldn't remember anything. Things were starting to spiral out of control, though I was still feeling on top of the world.

I had slept with pretty much every one of Ryan's friends at this point and quickly was known as the Cabanas slut. I would happily have sex with anyone who tried. I wanted to experience casual sex and rack up my sexual partners. It was such a thrill to me—almost a high.

I also enjoyed my reputation of being easy. Being so slutty was empowering, and I felt like I could actually let loose and be myself. When I was a small-town girl in Michigan, I always felt like I had to hold back because there were no other girls like me. When you're a stripper in Pensacola, you find a lot of girls willing to act promiscuous with you.

Not even a month of being single passed, though, before I decided to start dating another guy. I didn't want to be in a relationship, but there has always been a part of me that cannot bear to be alone. I was in no place to be faithful to someone or commit to them, but I needed someone who would be there for me so I wasn't lonely.

My dad, manger of Subway at the time, celebrated my birth
by announcing it on their sign in Houghton, Michigan.

Toddler me.

Was a Daddy's girl from day one.

*On the dance floor at my aunt's
wedding reception.*

*Self-timed photo of my family right
around the time my mom left.*

Jessica, my dad, and me outside my childhood home.

Old-time family photo taken in Wisconsin Dells,
where we vacationed each summer growing up.

Selfie taken while visiting my mom in South Carolina.

One of my middle school yearbook phot

My class of 2009 senior yearbook photo.

A selfie taken during my drug-dealer stage in the home of William.

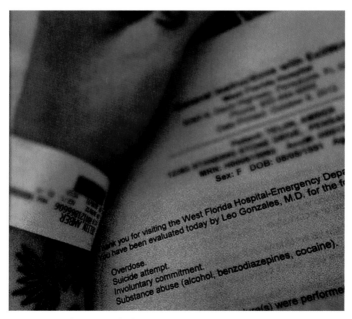

Paperwork I received after my suicide attempt. I posted this photo to social media to announce I would be trying to get sober— of course I wasn't successful for many more years.

All grown up, us three sisters are each others' best friends.

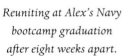

Reuniting at Alex's Navy bootcamp graduation after eight weeks apart.

Our reaction to eloping in Vegas!
We're married!

On stage (five weeks pregnant) where I won second place
in my bodybuilding competition.

Thirty-five weeks pregnant, waiting patiently
for our princess.

My dad, now the owner of the same Subway,
celebrating my daughter's birth on the same sign he
announced mine twenty-five years earlier.

I found the perfect guy to take advantage of, and his name was Seth.

Seth was a chubby white guy with a lot of facial and body hair. Although he had quite a few tattoos, everything else about him was the polar opposite of my usual type. I wasn't sexually attracted to him, but the fact that he seemed to worship me from day one was enough to spark my interest.

I had first met Seth at a GlowRage paint party, something I started doing a few weeks before dating him. GlowRage was a place where you would get high on molly and get covered in paint. Being that I was friends with the right people, I was one of the girls that got to work on stage throwing paint on other people. At least that was what I was supposed to be doing. Instead I spent the entire night shaking my ass and doing all my stripper moves in front of the giant crowd.

The first time I ever tried molly was at my first paint party. Jasmine introduced me to it in the bathroom stall. Molly is pretty much ecstasy but the pure version, also known as MDMA. I had a love-hate relationship with the drug. When I would take it, I would get so much energy and feel like the hottest woman in the entire world. I was unstoppable. I would not stop dancing for hours; it was all I wanted to do. However, once the party was over and we all stopped doing bumps of molly, the comedown was awful.

I was used to the bad comedowns from cocaine every day, but that was nothing compared to molly. I couldn't even talk when the drug was wearing off and the migraines were so bad. The worst part was that it always made me super suicidal. It would overwhelm me with regret and I felt worthless. But being the stupid drug addict I was, the high was worth it enough for me to start using it semi-regularly.

One of the perks of dating Seth was that he lived only minutes from Cabanas and Jasmine's place. From my mom's house, it always took at least a half hour to get into town, so I started living at Seth's house for days at a time until I eventually ran out of clothes and had to go back to my moms to get new ones.

Don't get me wrong, Seth was a nice guy, but clingy was an understatement. I was mean to him and never paid him much attention, but he still thought the world of me. I think maybe he knew there was no chance he'd date anyone like me again, so he kept holding on. It was painfully clear to everyone, and I imagine even him, that I was neither attracted to nor interested in him whatsoever. I kept dating him for a few months, however, so I could have a place to crash and someone to drive me around while I was intoxicated. Sometimes I'd even convince him to pay for my cocaine and that alone was enough for me to put up with anyone.

Seth dropped the L-bomb within a week of us getting to know each other. Of course, he said it while I was blackout drunk, so I said it back. He thought that I really meant it.

When I was drunk and high, I would spend time with him, but only at the bars. Most of that time involved me twerking and getting attention from other guys, sometimes even making out with other guys in front of him. Seth never got mad.

When I was sober (hungover), I wanted nothing to do with him, and I would avoid him the best I could. The only time he could get any words of affection out of me was when I was beyond fucked up. The same went for sex and even kissing.

I never let Seth touch me sober, but when I was blacked out, I would be too out of my mind to say no or to care. We never had sober sex once in our entire relationship. Any normal person would have left. Not Seth, though. He stayed.

One of the cool parts about being with Seth was that I could get away with whatever I wanted. He didn't dare try to tell me what to do because he knew I would leave in a heartbeat.

This was a breath of fresh air after dating Ryan and Tyler, two insanely, overly jealous, controlling boys.

One night I went to Cabanas without Seth but came back to his house afterward drunk. I was at Cabanas cheating on him with Ryan that night and someone at the bar texted Seth picture evidence.

What did Seth do? Nothing.

He showed me the evidence and I brushed it off like it was stupid, and we never spoke about it again. Although I knew I wasn't treating Seth right, it was a nice change to be in control for once. I didn't believe in love or relationships, so I didn't really care what happened.

The first relationship I knew was my mother, who let me down and left me after showing me I wasn't worthy of love. What would make some random guy ever be able to truly love me? This is what I told myself my entire teenage and adult years. I cheated on everyone I ever dated so I didn't feel stupid when they ended up cheating on or leaving me.

I was always one step ahead of hurting the person I was dating before they could hurt me. I was a rotten girlfriend, but in my head, it was my armor. You couldn't break my heart if I didn't have a heart to break. I became heartless and proud of it.

Even though I was technically dating Seth, I felt and acted single. I started becoming more and more out of control every single day. I knew the employees at Infinity Island could tell something was up with me. The only person that actually knew what I was up to was Jasmine, and that's because she was doing the exact same thing, though just not to the same extreme.

One night when we were tipsy, I decided to pee in the Infinity's sink. I posed as Jasmine laughed and took a picture to post on Instagram. When we came into work the next night, we were called into the manager's office. The owner of the club saw the Instagram post of me peeing in their sink and ordered the manager to fire us both. He told us that we'd violated the health code and that they could be sued because of us posting those pictures online. He explained that I had been given many chances at Infinity Island and that my chances were now up.

I had been called into the office previously for getting caught snorting coke with a customer. The worst part is that I snuck into the strip club office to do it, not knowing they had surveillance cameras. This was something else they said that they could be liable for if someone saw or found out.

I had also been in trouble for peeing while sitting at the bar during my shift. I was drunk one night and decided to just move my panties to the side and pee while sitting on the edge of the stool, letting my urine splash all over the floor. He didn't see me do it, just heard from another dancer that saw it, so I denied my way out of that one.

I didn't blame Infinity's for firing me; I was actually surprised I had lasted there so long. I was always leaving early with Jasmine, sneaking out the back door or making up bullshit excuses for why we had to leave early—the real reason always being that we needed more cocaine.

Jasmine and I were told to empty our lockers and leave immediately. We laughed off the incident, but on the inside, I was upset. Where was I going to work? We sat in my car and finally decided that we would try to get jobs at Nightshade Show Club, a strip club a mile down the road. All I knew about Nightshade was that it was considered the urban club of Pensacola. I was nervous that two new white girls would not be accepted by the other dancers. I was relieved when we got there and I saw the girls were ethnically mixed. I even recognized some of the girls who had previously worked at Infinity Island.

We spoke to the manager and both got jobs on the spot. When we danced there the first night, I learned I was going to love working at Nightshade more than ever. Not only were all of the girls on drugs, they all sold and bought drugs. All you had to do was ask the right girl and you could score some coke right then and there in the locker room. There was even a drug dealer who posed as a customer every night but was really there to make money off the drug-addicted strippers. Working at Nightshade was when my drug use hit an all-time high and my health hit an all-time low.

Within a couple weeks of working at Nightshade in late September, I had my first major health scare. I had always experienced chest pain after a night of bingeing on cocaine. I would feel it throughout the drug binge, but because I was so high, it never bothered me. When I would wake up the next morning, I would realize how severe the pains were. Sometimes I was convinced I would go into cardiac arrest at any moment, but I would simply eat a big meal and take it easy until the next day.

I also got my hands on a lot of molly once I started working at Nightshade. I would never spend my own money to buy it, though. I loved cocaine too much to cheat on it, but I was mixing molly with coke a few times a week. Jasmine would share hers with me since I would always share my coke with her. Customers also often gave it to me for free. The combination of the two drugs eventually caused my body to hit a breaking point.

One morning, waking up at Seth's, something didn't feel right. I had hardly eaten in the last three days and spent almost all of my waking hours on drugs. I tried to brush off the chest pain like I always did and went downstairs to smoke a cigarette. On the way to the patio, I decided to take a hit from a blunt Seth was smoking. I thought maybe a downer would calm the pain I was experiencing with my heart.

As I continued making my way out on the patio, everything went black. I could tell something very wrong was happening. I lost all control of my body, and my vision was gone for a good twenty seconds. I had no idea what was happening to me. I thought maybe this was finally death catching up with me. I could faintly hear Seth and his roommate yelling back and forth to each other to grab me a wet towel as I lay shaking on the patio floor.

Just as I felt like I was coming back to life and my body stopped jerking for a few seconds—BOOM! Another seizure hit and I lay there helplessly, praying it would end. The back-to-back seizures probably only lasted a minute or two but it felt like at least twenty minutes. I had never felt so powerless over my body. I was absolutely terrified.

Seth laid me in his bed while he went downstairs to talk to his roommate. My heart pain was severe, and I knew I needed to get to an emergency room. I was barely able to whisper, let alone yell to Seth downstairs. Getting up and walking was out of the question, and so I just lay there and waited for Seth to come back.

I fell asleep, and when I woke up I saw Seth staring at me. My high from the weed had faded but the heart pain and the feeling of death was still very real. I told him I needed to go to the hospital right away, that this was not something a fast-food burger and a little sleep could fix.

When you experience chest pain, you get VIP service at the emergency room. After they checked my vitals and did an EKG, a doctor came into the room to talk to me. He asked if I had been skipping my insulin shots. Confused, I told the doctor I did not have diabetes. He looked down at some papers and told me my blood sugar levels were that of a diabetic.

I told him that I thought smoking weed was what caused my seizures, but he assured me that it was my dangerous alcohol and hard drug use along with not eating that had brought them on. He was stern and serious as he spoke to me about how reckless I was being with my body. My blood pressure and heart rate were both at dangerous levels, and the doctor basically told me in a kind way that I was going to die if I didn't change something—and fast. He suggested a follow-up with my regular practitioner (I didn't have one) and to seek help from a therapist or recovery program.

After receiving fluids from an IV, I was free to leave the ER. All I wanted was to go home immediately and lie in bed. I got in my car once Seth took me back to his place and I told him I needed some time to be alone to take care of myself. Driving a vehicle after experiencing the seizures was terrifying. I was afraid that another one would happen without warning while I was behind the wheel. Funny how when I was blacked out, I never had this fear of crashing.

After briefly telling my mom what happened and her not even being somewhat concerned, I crawled into bed and cried the night away. I spent days at home sober and certain that I would never allow myself to be in that position again. However, when Thursday rolled around, I wanted to go back to work. I knew there was no possibility of me being sober at Nightshade, so I just told myself I wouldn't do any drugs.

I should've known that I could not simply drink without feeling the intense urge to use. Not even an hour into my shift, I was asking around for cocaine. I justified my decision to Jasmine by telling her it must've been all the molly that made me have a seizure, not the cocaine. I had been doing cocaine for a year without seizures, but molly was a new addiction and that's when the seizures happened. It sounded plausible, but I knew my body (and mind) could not handle more drugs—or even alcohol, for that matter. But as an addict, you find ways to justify your bad habits.

That weekend, I was right back into my normal routine of drinking and snorting dope. All thoughts of sobriety were out the window. Who was I kidding? There was no possible way for me to be a sober stripper, and I was having way too much fun partying every night.

The relationship I had with cocaine was the only relationship I would not ruin. Nothing made me as happy as the first line of the night. All of my anxiety and worries would fade away. Cocaine made me the happiest woman in the world. That was, until the baggie was empty—then I would be flooded with fear and panic.

The feeling of running out of coke while you're high on coke is something you can only understand if you've been there and done that. I even snorted bath salts when I couldn't find any more cocaine. I was desperate to recreate the cocaine high.

As the party continued, I did have some worries about my health in the back of my mind, but they were overpowered each day by the urge to use. When I was sober, I could feel all of the emotions and depression that consumed me, but when I was using, all of my issues went away. I was numb.

Two weeks after my back-to-back seizures, on October 8, 2012, I got the biggest wake-up call I could possibly get.

The day started out like any other. I woke up at three in the afternoon and started getting ready for work. I had a bottle of Fireball with a small amount of whiskey left in my dancer bag but decided to stop at the liquor store before work to grab another bottle. I picked up a bottle of vodka before heading to Destiny's house to buy a gram of blow for the night ahead.

I always got to the strip club a good half hour before my shift started so I had time to change into my tiny stripper outfit, put on my fishnets and stilettos, fix my hair and makeup, and then get thoroughly tipsy. Once Jasmine and I were ready, we would take turns chugging straight liquor from whatever bottle I brought with me to work, then we'd make our way to the bathroom to snort some lines. This was followed by chain-smoking until our first roll call of the night. This always ensured the night would be off to a fabulous start.

That night, Kate, who also worked at Nightshade, gave me a couple of Xanax in exchange for a couple bumps of coke. Even though I rarely did pills, I obliged. I knew from the past that every time I took Xanax while drinking was a guarantee that I would completely black out. Not that it was anything out of the ordinary, but along with the blackout, the pill would make me very angry and emotional.

By the time I had finished my first gram of coke of the night, I was desperate for more, per usual. I had to wait an entire hour for Destiny to make it to Nightshade because none of the dancers had any to sell that night. Trying not to come down from my high, I crushed up a Xanax in the bathroom and snorted it, desperate for any kind of drug.

By the time Destiny made it to Nightshade, I was already messed up out of my mind on vodka, tequila, whiskey, Xanax, and coke; but I still needed more cocaine.

There could never be enough cocaine.

I started feeling more depressed than usual about everything in my life. Out of nowhere I was missing Tyler terribly, texting him audio clips of a song a stripper was dancing to called "Neva End" by Future, which used to be "our song."

Sure, I had Seth, but because I had zero feelings invested in him, he didn't make me feel any less alone. I started thinking about my abortion and how stupid I was for having it. It was a fast mental downward spiral. I figured I'd just snort the new gram I had bought and that it would fix my problems, but within another hour I was in a state of severe depression.

When the second gram of the night ran out, I decided to leave work. I called for Seth to pick me up since he had dropped me off that night. I was visibly upset and told him to just drive me to my car at his house, but on the way there I had another idea.

I told Seth to let me run into Walgreens so I could buy a pack of cigarettes. I texted Jasmine, Tyler, my sisters, and my dad before walking inside. The text was something to the effect that I loved them so much but couldn't take life anymore.

I grabbed a bottle of sleeping pills off the shelves and went to the register. It was almost like I hit a point of calm. I was content with my decision. I knew I was a waste of life. No one would ever love me, and I would never be truly happy. I was ready to die. I stood at the garbage can outside of Walgreens and started swallowing as many pills as I could before Seth saw and ran over to stop me. He carried me to the car and started yelling at me, asking me what I had done. I told him I wanted to die and proceeded to swallow more pills while he just watched.

That's when the memories start to go black.

After I passed out and started foaming at the mouth in his passenger seat, Seth sped as fast as he could to the nearest emergency room. I guess they wheeled me into the hospital as I was unconscious and could not walk.

I can recall doctors all around me in a rush asking me repeatedly what I had taken that night. With my slurred speech of barely being conscious, I told them everything that was in my system. I remember crying about how my mom didn't love me when they asked me why I wanted to hurt myself. Then I remember the pain of them putting in a catheter. All of these memories are hazy and foggy, like how you recall a dream. I don't remember anything else of that night, but I do remember thinking I was on my way to death.

KARMEN   AMBER VAN DE BUNT

When I woke up the next afternoon, it took me a while to recall what had happened the night before. I instantly felt embarrassed, but I had more important things to worry about—like where the hell I was. I looked at the room around me; there was nothing in it. I was in an empty room with white concrete walls. The only thing in the room was a tray of food on the floor and my hospital bed. I was dressed in nothing but a cloth gown and that's when I realized I had no piercings in. My lip rings, nose ring, belly button ring, and nipple rings were all missing. I got up and went to leave the room when I realized I was locked inside.

Was I in jail? I started to panic, not knowing when someone would come for me.

There was a window on the door and I started to frantically pound on it while yelling for someone to come help me. A police officer came to the door and told me I was being held by the Baker Act. This consisted of being able to hold involuntary patients for mental health evaluations. I asked for my phone and was denied. I told him I had to use the bathroom, and he told me he would have to walk me there and monitor me to make sure I wasn't hurting myself. This is the same reason I was placed in an empty room and had my piercings removed. They didn't want to provide me with anything sharp that I could possibly try to harm myself with.

I felt like a crazy person and wanted to leave immediately. I asked when I was allowed to call my family and he said my family had already been called by my boyfriend, who was still waiting in the lobby. I was told I would not be released until they had talked to my friends or family to evaluate my mental state. I also got to speak to a doctor myself, and I lied through my teeth telling them I was not depressed or suicidal.

All I wished at that moment was that I really had died, because this was a living nightmare. I could be held for up to five days in this empty room, which I was certain would make me go legitimately psychotic if I hadn't already.

The doctor seemed to believe my story that I was simply just way too drunk and didn't remember taking all of the sleeping pills. He said if my story checked out with my friends and family that I would be free to leave. Sure enough, I was leaving the hospital a few hours later, less than twenty-four hours after being admitted. All I could think was "idiots" as they told me I could leave. How could trained doctors not see something was seriously wrong with me? I was thankful for their naivety, however, and was ready to leave.

When I walked through the door to the waiting room, I was pleasantly surprised to see Jasmine, Seth, and Kate all waiting for me. They looked like they were on the verge of tears when they saw me. We all had a long group hug and Jasmine scolded me to never be stupid like that again. We had to go to a different section of the hospital so I could fill out some paperwork and speak with another doctor before being fully discharged.

The first page of my paperwork had all of my patient information, followed by:

> You have been evaluated today by Leo Gonzales, MD, for the following:
>
> Overdose.
> Suicide attempt.
> Involuntary commitment.
> Substance abuse (alcohol, benzodiazepines, cocaine).

There was a long list afterward of the procedures that had been performed during my emergency stay. It didn't feel real that this had actually happened to me. I had so much paperwork to do before my nightmare was over and I would be allowed to leave.

The process felt like it took forever, and I had a lot of waiting time. I used it to go through all the texts on my phone. I had messages from Tyler and Jasmine from the night before questioning my weird goodbye text. Both of my sisters and my dad had sent me sweet texts letting me know how much they loved me, all which were sent that morning. I knew that meant they knew exactly what had happened to me.

Seth told me that my stepdad, mom, brother, and sister Amanda had all been at the hospital earlier that morning to try to visit me. Seth called Amanda countless times in the middle of the night until one call finally woke her up and he could let her know what had happened. When they tried to visit me, the doctor told them they would not be allowed to speak to me until I was evaluated, so they had no choice but to go back home.

I felt stupid but texted back everyone in my family to let them know I was being released from the hospital and that I was okay, to which they seemed relieved. That's when I realized I had no messages from my mother.

Shocking.

When I finally left the hospital and drove back to my mom's house, my sister filled me in on what had happened the night before.

When Seth woke Amanda up to let her know I had over-dosed, she ran in a panic to my mom's room to let them know what was going on. She said my stepdad hopped right out of bed and woke up my brother so they could leave immediately, but then there was my mother, bitching that it was the middle of the night and that no one should talk to her before she had her coffee.

That's when my mom made herself a cup and sat on her computer scrolling through Facebook to "wake up" before she could leave. Meanwhile, she knew her daughter was in the hospital, barely clinging to life. The rest of the family could not believe she was being so selfish and careless. The icing on the cake was that when she was done with her coffee, she had to go do her hair before leaving the house. Mind you, this is before anyone knew whether I was alive or dead. The hospital couldn't tell anybody any status on my health until I was stabilized.

What did my "mother" do? She took her sweet damn time while complaining about how tired she was. I shouldn't have been surprised by this information, as she had shown for years how little she actually cared about her children, but it definitely was one of the times she had made me feel the worst. The woman who gave birth to me thought coffee, Facebook, and doing her hair were more urgent than rushing to be by her dying child in the emergency room.

I was happy to be in my own bed, not the hospital, but was so depressed with the information Amanda had just told me. As I lay in bed, replaying the images in my head of my mom not caring about me the night before, a text from my dad popped up.

"Well, are you going to come outside or what?"

I yelled to Amanda as I ran outside barefoot. I couldn't believe that my dad's car was in the driveway. I ran over to my dad and hugged him so tightly. That's when my sister Jessica hopped out of the vehicle too. I jumped on her and told them how happy I was to see them.

My dad said as soon as Amanda had told him what happened, he got into his car and drove across the country to come see me. On the way down, he picked up my sister from her dorm room at college. The negative thoughts about my mom vanished when I saw how much my dad and sisters cared about me.

I could always count on my daddy to be there for me.

He told me and Amanda to pack a bag because we were going to stay in a penthouse suite on the beach. It was a beautiful gated resort and our room was basically like a three-bedroom

 Amber van de Bunt

apartment. Our family had never stayed at such a beautiful place, but it was exactly what I needed. That week with my family reminded me of all of the things in my life that I had to live for.

My dad has never been one to confront issues or to get personal, so all he really said about the hospital situation were things like:

"What were you thinking, honey?"

"You can't be doing stuff like that."

"You need to stop all of the drugs and drinking."

I assured him I had learned my lesson, even though I knew I probably hadn't. Once the weekend rolled around, I told him I had to go to work to get money and he handed me a hundred-dollar bill to stay at the penthouse with our family. My dad tried very hard to help heal me, and if there's any person who could do so, it would be him. But drug addictions are very powerful things.

When my dad left town to drive back to Michigan, he took my little sister with him. I was sad at the time but quickly realized that the best thing for her was not to be around my mother. I told my dad I would quit the drugs and drinking and was determined to make it in sobriety this time. I took out my notebook and made a plan that I even uploaded to the Internet to show people I was serious this time.

FEEL BETTER PLAN

Drinks: water, tea, milk

Foods: clean eating only—NO JUNK!

(soup, fruits, veggies, oats, bran cereal, oats, nuts, cheese, etc.)

high fiber—low fat

Exercise: (Abs, squats/lunges, pushups) + daily walk/jog when not dancing—daily multivitamin, biotin, immune system pill, and iron pill

NO GETTING WASTED AND NO DRUGS

AFTER THE OVERDOSE, I stayed sober for six days before I was back partying and working at the strip club. Not even being seconds away from death was enough for me to stay sober. The sad part is I had really attempted to stay clean. I had written on social media that I needed to stop drinking and doing drugs, but when I would be sitting at home all alone in my depression, it was all I wanted to turn to. It was like I no longer was in control of myself. Cocaine was completely in control of me.

I knew I should never have gotten off my Prozac in the months prior and that it probably contributed to my suicide attempt and heavy drug use, so I made the positive decision to visit a doctor to get back on it. I'd spent all my high school years refusing and skipping pills that my dad would beg me to take, and now here I was dying to get back on it. It is surprising what one small pill can do for your well-being. When I saw they were actually working, and that now I wasn't being forced onto them, I became an antidepressant advocate. I never wanted to get off medication as long as I lived. Mostly out of fear I would end up back in the hospital—or worse.

Even though I was making progress on the Prozac, I continued to party over the next few weeks. The small clarity that the meds were giving me told me I needed a change of scenery. I had thought that starting over in Pensacola would bring me happiness, but all it brought me was a drug addiction, an abortion, and some near-death experiences. Of course, these were all due to my own negligence, but in my head I just needed to start over again and things would be okay.

It also didn't help me at all mentally when I was living with such a toxic human being. When my mom wasn't screaming and having emotional meltdowns, she was being the most offensive "mother" you could imagine. This woman even had the nerve to pop her head into my room one day about a month after my overdose to tell me, "I got you a Christmas present today, so don't kill yourself until after the holidays!" followed by a laugh. I had enough of waiting around for her to be a mother, and I considered moving back to Michigan, but I knew there was nothing there for me. The only other place I could move to was California.

That is, if I decided to actually pursue my one true desire of being a porn star.

Porn Star Dreams

I CAN'T EVEN TELL you how many different websites and companies I looked at when I started to seriously consider doing porn. A lot of the companies told me I needed to have an agent, but I wasn't sure if I was ready for that commitment. I wanted to test the waters first to see if porn was all that I hoped it would be.

When I was eighteen—a blonde and tattoo-less teen— Reality Kings in Miami offered me a girl/girl scene and a boy/girl scene taking place in a nightclub, so I thought I'd reconnect with them and see if they'd still make me that offer. I went to their email from three years prior and sent a reply telling them I was interested in finally making it happen.

"Hey, I don't know if you remember me, but we talked about me shooting for *Molly's Life* and *In The VIP*. Haha, it's been about two years…I'm STILL interested :) Love, Carmen"

Clearly, I was quite the professional inquirer. They turned me down when they saw that I had heavily tattooed myself in the interim, so that idea was out.

Feeling frustrated about being rejected, I Googled "tattoo porn." How had I never heard of BurningAngel.com? It was a porn site full of pierced and tattooed women with colored hair. I felt like it was meant to be as soon as I discovered the site.

I was relieved I wouldn't be forced to go back to my natural hair color, which I considered "boring." I filled out the model application on their website and anxiously waited for a reply. To my surprise, I would have an email the next morning with an answer, and that email would forever change my life.

They were interested!

They asked me some questions, mostly about what I would be willing to shoot for them. They also asked me to send some current photos. I was told I had to submit nude photos from the front, side, and back. They also needed a photo of me holding a piece of paper with my name and the date on it. I assumed this was due to girls being flown out who ended up looking nothing like their pictures.

After immediately doing my hair and makeup, I set up my self-timer to take the required shots. I told them I would be willing to do girl/girl shoots and boy/girl shoots. With my email sent, all I could think about was how I would be graduating from stripper to porn star very soon. After a few more emails were exchanged, we set up the dates I would be coming to Los Angeles. The company's "Commander in Chief" sent over a flight agreement document. It stated that I would be responsible for paying them back for my round-trip flight.

I was a little bummed that I had to pay for my own flight, but it was more about the experience than the money for me at that point. I had dreamt of being a porn star for so many years and I was actually about to make it happen. I signed the document and later that week they sent me my flight information. In November 18 through 22, I would be in California living out my dreams.

Soon I discovered the owner of the website, Joanna Angel. She sent me a welcome email explaining the two shoots I would be doing. The email told me who I was going to be working with, what sites I would be working for, and what I needed to bring with me in my suitcase. The first thing I did was Google her. She was a hot, tiny brunette with pink streaks in her hair and a body covered in beautiful colorful art. I was super excited when I learned I would be staying in her guest bedroom for the duration of the trip. The information in the email made me even more excited.

"You will be shooting 2 boy/girl scenes for BurningAngel. com with a rate of $900 each. November 19 you will be shooting with Danny Wylde. There will be a makeup artist on set and wardrobe will be provided. November 21 you will be shooting a POV with Mr. Pete. Look on POVPUNX.com to see what they are like. The clothing for those scenes is usually simple. Wifebeaters, shorts, bras and panties, a cute bathing suit. Hair/ Makeup will be provided.

"The scenes will be simple with a little bit of dialogue but no script or anything. Also, PLEASE bring a copy of your STD test. Looking forward to meeting you. Xoxox, Joanna Angel"

I spent the rest of that day watching every trailer on the Burning Angel website and researching both of the male talents I would be working with. I wanted to get as much information as I could to make sure I shot the best scenes possible.

I probably watched over one hundred trailers that day alone and continued to watch them until the morning of my first shoot. Danny Wylde was a tall, skinny blond boy with no tattoos—not exactly the type of guy I thought I would be shooting with for a tattoo porn site. Mr. Pete was more of what I was expecting physically—everything about him screamed bad boy. He had a shaved head, pierced ears, and tattoos down his arms.

On the morning of my flight, I started getting major butterflies. Part of me thought about backing out and not going to the airport. I wanted to do porn so badly, but the reality—that if I got on the plane, I would for sure have to go through with my decision—was scary. I wasn't afraid of shooting the actual scenes, although I was quite nervous for that part.

My main concern was my dad.

I had been my daddy's little girl from the moment I was born. He was very strict, and I knew how much I had already disappointed him with all of my acting out. There was also a definite chance of him disowning me if he found out I was a porn star. This dilemma had held me back since I was eighteen. I knew it was something I really wanted to do, but I kept trying to be happy with just web-camming, then just stripping—but it wasn't satisfying me. I wanted more. I wanted the fame, the money, and the sexual experiences that only porn could provide me.

As much as I loved my dad, I was tired of holding back in fear of how he would react. It was my life and I wanted to make myself happy. I knew I would always regret not doing porn if I didn't at least experience it somewhat. This was a perfect opportunity for me.

I only had to shoot two scenes, and if I didn't like it I never had to do it again. Plus, I thought maybe there was a chance he would never find out. I had Seth drive me to the airport as I kept telling him I wasn't sure if I could go through with this. When we were almost to the airport, I spotted a liquor store.

"STOP THERE! Now!"

I ran inside and got eight mini bottles of Fireball. If I got too nervous before one of the shoots, I could do a few shots to take the edge off. When I hopped back into the car I decided to just drink one now for good measure and put the other seven in my suitcase for California. After that, I had no problem getting on my flight.

I landed in Los Angeles that afternoon with more nerves than I had ever experienced. Joanna told me to take a shuttle to the train station, where she would pick me up. I had never taken a shuttle, let alone a train before, so I was super nervous. I had no idea what I was doing and after already texting Joanna multiple times, I decided I could figure it out on my own. I didn't want to annoy her before she had even met me.

I was proud of myself when I reached the destination I was supposed to be at a couple of hours later. Joanna called me saying she would be pulling up in a black truck any minute. I grabbed my suitcase and carry-on bag and waited on the sidewalk for her arrival. I had no idea what to expect.

What were we supposed to talk about? I was awful at making conversation with people I already knew and even worse with strangers. I got in and couldn't believe I was in the car with a porn star. I felt a bit creepy because I had watched so many scenes of her on Burning Angel. I knew what every part of her body looked like under her clothes. Of course, I never told her any of this and played it off like I didn't really know who she was.

Joanna informed me that before we went to her house for the night, we would have to stop by the shooting location. It was a very old building with three floors. Little did I know one day I would be shooting a Waka Flocka Flame music video in that very same location.

Right when we walked in, I saw two completely naked girls and a naked man. They were having a conversation, laughing with each other as if they were fully clothed. Joanna told them it was time to get back to filming and I watched both girls take a baby wipe and wipe their vaginas before running back over to the set. As the director said "action," the girls started making very loud moans out of nowhere.

Observing this for the first time was so bizarre to me. I couldn't believe that this was going to be me in just twenty-four hours. They seemed so confident with no cares in the world, while I was shaking even observing their scene.

This was the first time I had ever watched people have sex right in front of me. They didn't care that Joanna and I were sitting back and watching, they didn't pay us any attention. Once the male talent came over both of their faces, the director yelled cut and the girls started laughing. They wiped the cum off their faces, grabbed some snacks off the table, and started talking about how great the scene was.

One of the girls noticed I was sitting back watching and asked if I was going to be shooting for Burning Angel. I told her yes and that I was a little nervous. She said, "Don't be nervous! It's so much fun, you'll love it."

I hoped she was right, because there was no turning back now.

As I lay in Joanna's guest bedroom later that night, I could not get my mind to stop racing. She told me to be up and ready at 10:00 a.m. to get to hair and makeup on time. How was I supposed to sleep knowing I would be shooting my first porno in the morning? I sat there thinking how weird it was that I was going to be having sex so early in the day.

I always assumed porn shoots took place late at night. Isn't that normally when people had sex? I quickly reminded myself that this wasn't normal life anymore. Later down the road, I would be thankful for a 10:00 a.m. call time; some directors would want me there as early as 6:00 a.m.

I lay there in the dark thinking about every possible scenario for the next day, and after a couple hours passed, I finally fell asleep. It was November 19, 2012—the first day I would be in a pornographic film. The first thing my makeup artist asked me was if she could take a before-and-after picture of me for her Instagram. I obliged, not wanting to piss off the person who was supposed to be making me look hot. If I would've known she was going to be selling these pictures (along with countless other porn stars' pictures) to multiple websites, I would've said no.

I had two huge zits above my upper lip that I had been picking at all week, trying to get them to go away, but this only made open wounds that had turned into scabs by the morning of my shoot. I asked if she would just put concealer on my blemishes for the before picture, but she assured me that this would make the before-and-after pictures even better.

Thinking that no one I knew would see her Instagram page, I went along with it. The reality was that "Porn Stars Without Makeup" links would be viral all over the Internet, and all of my old friends would be sending me the links to let me know about it.

I spent a lot of time reading the comments on all of these websites. Many people commented that I had "meth face," and some even claimed I had a herpes outbreak on my face. I was mortified at the whole experience and so was the rest of the adult industry. This makeup artist was, thankfully, never used by any director or porn star again.

My hot pink hair was done in bouncy curls and I had a gorgeous smoky eye with hot pink lips. Joanna handed me my wardrobe for the shoot, which consisted of a crop top and matching leggings. I absolutely loved the outfit. The material was pink with black stripes and made out of a silky fabric. I went to the bathroom to take selfies and the director knocked on the door telling me it was time to take "pretty girls"—which is what they called the solo photos. They were taken in various stages of dressed and undressed.

Next up were the "sex stills," which were shots taken before or after the sex scene, depending on what company you were shooting for. You would pose for blowjob stills, stills of each position you were doing in the scene, and lastly "pop-shot photos," which were of the cum shot. If the stills were done before the scene, the pop-shot pictures weren't actual cum. The director or production assistant (PA) would squirt pumps of Cetaphil cleanser onto the actresses' face, which resembled the same color and consistency as semen. She would then pose with the dick, acting as if she had just gotten a real facial.

Even if the sex stills were taken after the sex scene, the majority of the time we still got Cetaphil to the face. This was due to the male talent's load not being impressive or if the girl had already eaten it off her face for the end of the scene. The director recommended that I do the sex stills first so I could get more comfortable before the actual scene, and I agreed.

As I walked onto the set for pretty girls, my whole body was shaking uncontrollably. Never in my life had I experienced anything like that before. It made it pretty hard to play it off like I wasn't nervous.

The director walked me through certain poses he wanted from me and I continued to shake the entire time. It wasn't until Danny Wylde's dick touched my mouth that I stopped shaking.

Once we were shooting the sex stills, my body slowly relaxed and I was getting eager for the actual scene.

With all of the pictures done, the director told me he just had to switch cameras and we would be ready to film the scene. I noticed Joanna Angel was sitting at a table behind the bright lights, observing. With the pressure of her watching me, I knew I had to do my absolute best. I really wanted to impress her.

I was told that the scene would be thirty minutes long, and I began to panic. The guys I had been with up to this point were lucky to last five. What was I supposed to do for a half hour? I knew we had four sex positions and a blowjob to get through, so I made a quick mental note: if all else fails, suck his dick.

The cameras started rolling and I was instructed to flirt with the camera and do a strip tease until Danny walked into frame. Those two minutes felt like an eternity. I felt like I was doing the same thing over and over again. Then Danny walked over to me. He began kissing down my body, then pulled my pants down with his mouth and started licking my ass. This was actually exciting, and I was legitimately turned on.

After watching the girls shoot their scene yesterday, I wondered if it was all just an act, but it was different for me. I enthusiastically dropped to my knees to give him the best blowjob of his life.

He took my top off and blindfolded me and choked me with it throughout the scene. Five minutes into the scene, I had already forgotten the camera was filming us, and before I knew it, Danny was cumming on my face. A few moments later, everyone on set was clapping for me.

"Are you sure this is your first time shooting?" Joanna asked me.

I knew I was going to love doing porn, but I had no idea I would be such a natural at it. I grabbed a baby wipe like I had seen the girls do yesterday and wiped the cum off my face, but there was no wiping off the smile. When Joanna drove me home that evening, she kept complimenting me on how well I did. I was on top of the world, but I was disappointed that I would not be doing anything the following day, and I knew the day after would be the second and final shoot of my trip.

It was the morning of November 21, and I hopped in the shower to make sure I was perfectly shaved for the shoot. I was told to do my own hair and makeup but as soon as I finished, I received a text from Joanna saying a makeup artist was going to stop by her place to do touch-ups on me to make sure I looked camera-ready. She recurled my hair, touched up my makeup quickly, and left.

Joanna was at work, and I was sitting around her apartment by myself waiting on Mr. Pete to show up. When he texted me that he would arrive in ten minutes, butterflies returned to my belly.

This seemed a lot different than yesterday's shoot. When I was in the studio, there were so many people around that it didn't feel awkward, but now I was alone at someone else's house about to shoot a porno with a guy I had never met.

This is when the bottles of Fireball came to the rescue. I drank two of the mini bottles, and next thing I knew he was knocking at the door. He looked exactly like his pictures. I asked him about the shoot and he briefly talked over what we would be doing.

Before I knew it, he pulled down his pants and had me suck his dick. It was the first uncircumcised penis I had ever seen, but I acted like it was normal for me. A few moments later we were having sex on the couch. I kept glancing around the room, noticing that there was no camera in sight. When I finally said something, he told me he had to get the equipment from the car and went downstairs to grab it.

Was this normal? I had just had sex with the male talent, and it wasn't even for the camera. Also, were uncircumcised penises the same as circumcised penises? I wasn't sure what I was supposed to do with it. I redressed myself as I waited for him to come back. We did quick dialogue for the scene before we started having sex again, this time on camera.

The story for the scene was that Mr. Pete was my driver, and I was late coming out to the car. He knocked on my door and I told him to come inside while I got ready. I then seduced him by bending over and finally crawling over to his lap and unbuttoning his pants. I couldn't believe I was acting out one of these cheesy porno scenarios everyone always made fun of. Once again, though, I relaxed as I started the blowjob and felt much more comfortable.

We had an amazing sex scene, but it was much different shooting POV, point of view, rather than having a director. With a director filming the scene, the male talent does as much of the work as the female talent, if not more. With a POV scene, the girl is left to do ALL of the work because the male has to hold the camera. My legs burned from riding his cock for so long, and just when I thought I couldn't do it any longer, he signaled for me to get down to swallow his cum.

My second porno was complete, and I was exhausted. Mr. Pete told me it was a great scene and that Joanna was going to be very happy with it. He packed up his equipment and left. I called my boyfriend to let him know how awesome the scene went and that I would be home tomorrow.

I spent the entire flight back home to Florida thinking about my porn experience. I was so anxious for my videos to come out so I could watch them. I wanted to shoot so many more scenes. I loved getting my hair and makeup done, I loved having my photo taken, and I loved having sex on camera. This was most definitely my calling, and I spent the next few weeks applying to every agency I could come across online.

It was decided. I was going to pursue an actual career as a porn star.

I felt like a rock star when I was back in Pensacola. Everyone had known what I went to California to do, and I was not shy about it. My job at Nightshade was fun, and I couldn't imagine life without Jasmine—but my heart was calling me to Los Angeles. How could I deny myself the career that was meant for me? Sure, it isn't your ordinary career, but some people are really good at being doctors and others are just really good at sucking dick. I knew it was the right choice for me.

My dip into the porn industry even got me out of a DUI that first week back in Pensacola. After leaving Cabanas, I tried to drive myself home. I got about five miles before being pulled over. I don't remember anything before seeing the cop lights pulling me over.

I quickly pulled into a fast food parking lot and waited for the cop to come talk to me. How stupid was I to drive so fucked up? I was supposed to be leaving for Los Angeles again soon. I was terrified now that I'd be stuck in jail.

The cop asked me if I had been drinking because I apparently was swerving in and out of my lane. I told him I'd had a few drinks but added, "I'm Karmen Karma. I do porn."

This sounds absolutely ridiculous, but the cop never used a breathalyzer on me or went any further with delivering consequences. Instead, he was clearly intrigued by my career and asked me questions about the porn industry. He asked if I had a friend who could pick me up, and I called Jasmine immediately—even though Jasmine didn't have a valid license at the time thanks to her own previous DUI.

So here I was, flirting my way out of a DUI, talking about doing porn, and the cop lets someone without a license (and who has also been drinking) drive me home. Jasmine is still convinced to this day that I gave the cop a blowjob to get out of the DUI, but I did not.

But I totally would have if he'd suggested it.

The last thing I needed was *another* DUI. With all of my blacked-out driving, I somehow never once got in trouble in Florida. I am so lucky to be alive after all of my irresponsible choices. You would think after that close call that I quit drinking and driving—at least for a while, right?

Wrong.

It was December, and I continued to strip for a few weeks until I flew back to Michigan to spend Christmas with my family. Staying in Florida with my mom was not an option; she never felt like family. My dad and my sisters were, and always will be, my world.

My sisters knew about the trip to Los Angeles, but we never talked about the details. Thankfully they were trustworthy, and I knew they would never tell my dad what I was up to. I decided that after the holidays, when I flew back to Florida, I would start my real porn career by joining an adult agency in California. I spent a lot of time doing my research, and I finally narrowed it down to a few that I would apply to.

After talking to three different agencies who were happy to accept me, I finally settled on California Modeling. The reason I chose them was that they represented a girl named Christy Mack. Christy was one of the top porn stars and was also covered in tattoos. If they could help her get so successful, I had faith in them to help put me on the same path.

The only bad news was that all three agencies told me I had to dye my hair to a natural color. I thought dying my hair to my natural color would make me "plain," but porn was more important than my hair color, and by the end of the week I had my natural brown locks again.

Christmas and New Year's had passed, and it was time to put my plan into action. I talked on the phone with my agent, Jackson, to figure out a good day for me to fly to California now that I had money saved from my other porn scenes and could afford my own ticket.

He wanted me to fly out that week, and I was a both shocked and pleased that he wanted me to come so soon. I agreed. I told him I would send him my flight information after booking the ticket. It was a Friday afternoon and I booked my flight for Monday morning. I wasn't sure how long I would want to stay there, so I only bought a one-way ticket.

With only three days left in Pensacola, I decided to make the most of it. On Friday night I usually worked at Nightshade, but I wanted to spend one last night at Cabanas before I left. I also wanted to hang out with Ryan one last time. For some odd reason, after all of the bullshit he put me through, I couldn't stop hanging out with him. It would still be a few more years before I formed any sort of respect for myself.

Like any other night Ryan and I hung out, we would make our rounds at the bars and strip clubs before drunkenly fucking in his Tahoe. This night would be much different, though.

I knew this was likely the last night I would ever get to see Ryan, so I wanted to go all out. I lost track of how many shots I'd done within the first hour. All I can remember is his begging me not to "leave him" and go to California.

I woke up in a hotel room next to Evan, Ryan's cousin. I had no recollection of even running into him the night before. I looked over at the other side of the room and there was Ryan sleeping on the other bed. I yelled "what the fuck?" and both cousins woke up. They soon began laughing when they realized I had no memory of even coming to the hotel. Per usual, I asked about everything that had happened the night before. Usually

I was told I had taken my top off at Cabanas or danced naked on the bar, but the first thing I heard out of Ryan's mouth stunned me.

"Well, you were fucking my cousin!" he said, sounding pissed off.

I looked over at Evan to see if this information was true or not.

"Dude, you told me to! That's why you brought me here!" he said.

I was highly confused, listening to them bicker back and forth, until I found out there was a threesome that had happened. Of course, Ryan had initiated it—that was no surprise. And even less surprising was that Ryan got hard feelings during the middle of the ordeal. It sounded a lot like the Brandon threesome, except without me getting punched in the face afterward—or at least I assumed.

As hard as I tried, I couldn't remember having sex with anyone. Usually having sex sobered me up enough to remember it the next day. I had a bad feeling in the pit of my stomach, but I was so hungover that the nausea in my stomach overruled the bad feeling. Ryan dropped me off at my car, and I drove home to sleep the rest of the day away.

Fast-forward to me living in California, I get a text message out of the blue from Ryan saying he misses me. I had a boyfriend at the time, but I was bored and decided to reply to him anyway. He told me how much he missed fucking me, and that all he had were our pictures and videos to remember me by. That's when he had the nerve to send me the worst video I have ever watched.

It was a video of the threesome in the hotel room. It was a two-minute video of me passed out, eyes closed, and silent while they fucked me and shoved their dicks in my mouth. The only noise I made the entire video was a drunken groan that only someone who was about to die of alcohol poisoning could make. I watched in horror as they took advantage of me. The most sickening part was listening to their conversation. It was completely clear they were fully aware I was incoherent.

"Dude, you can cum in her," Ryan said. "She's on birth control. Don't worry about it."

I couldn't believe they had the nerve to have sex with me while I was passed out. I felt so violated. Beyond that, I couldn't believe Ryan thought this video was okay to send to me. There was no way any person could watch this video and think it was consensual sex.

I never spoke to him again.

It took me a couple years to come to terms with the fact that I was raped that night, and many others. I always brushed things off as my fault. That I shouldn't have been so drunk, that I should've been meaner when I said "no." Part of me still struggles not to blame myself. If I wasn't out getting wasted, I wouldn't have been so easily taken advantage of. I'm not sure how many times things like this had happened to me when blacking out was a regular part of my life, but I'm sure it's more than I'd like to know.

I woke up later that night still hungover and feeling uneasy about the night before. I checked my phone and had multiple texts from Jasmine. She knew it was the last night that I could party before going back to Los Angeles. I kept telling her how hungover I was and that I truly didn't feel like going out—a very rare occurrence. Jasmine would not take no for an answer, and finally I told her I would start getting ready for another wild night out.

We started our night like any other night together: I would drive to her house and we would have her drug dealer come over. After doing a few lines each and drinking a few shots, we would drive into town. We decided to stop at the strip clubs first before heading over to Cabanas. We said hi to all the girls at

Nightshade then walked over to Scandal's to say hi to our friend Johnny, who was bartending.

Two shots of vodka at Scandal's later, and the next thing I knew I was having sex with the club manager in their VIP room. He was an unattractive, middle-aged man and it was only 10:00 p.m., so that's how my night was going, apparently. Jasmine, in disbelief but not shocked anymore by my poor sexual choices, told me it was time to leave and go to Cabanas.

We danced, drank, and snorted lines in the bathroom until the bar closed at 2:00 a.m. For us the night was just beginning though, and I made sure to text Destiny to meet us at Bedlams so we could get another gram of coke. By the time we left Bedlams, it was close to five in the morning and we were thoroughly trashed. Johnny was having people over for an after-after-party, and because we knew he was a huge cokehead, we were there. The sun was already up but we were partying like it was still nighttime.

Johnny laid out a giant mirror that six or seven of us kept taking turns doing lines off of for a couple hours. By 8:00 a.m., my nose could not snort any more drugs, which happened once in a while. Occasionally I would snort so much coke that my nose literally would not take in more. It was frustrating, but it only ever occurred after I had done at least three or four grams by myself, so it was probably a pretty good warning sign that I should stop before I died.

The coke was running low and Jasmine and I were starting to come down—the worst feeling in the world. We decided it was time to drive to her house and get some sleep. Johnny's house was only fifteen minutes away, but in the fucked-up state I was in, I shouldn't have even been functioning, let alone operating a vehicle.

I have no memory of the drive home until Jasmine and I were fighting, pressing buttons on my music player in the car. She kept trying to turn off the 2 Chainz song I wanted to listen to and whenever she would press the arrow to skip to the next song, I would press the back arrow to bring it right back. We were laughing as we changed the music and I wasn't even paying attention to the road.

Boom. That's when we got into an accident.

The car that I had smacked into driving fifty miles an hour was at a complete stop ahead of me, and I had no idea what to do. Jasmine suggested we just run and when I tried to drive, I could hear my front bumper scraping the road. An elderly woman got out of her car and I knew I couldn't try to drive away now. My car had pink rims, for God's sake. I would be very easy to track down if I did a hit-and-run.

The old woman slowly walked over to me and asked me how to dial 911 on her cell phone. This poor lady was just starting her Sunday morning—probably going to church—while I was still in party mode from the night before.

A cop quickly arrived and instructed us to pull over on the side of the road, which I could not do until he ripped off my hanging bumper. While the officer got the old woman's story, Jasmine and I were taking selfies in my car. I instantly uploaded a photo to Facebook with the caption, "Pulled over waiting to see if I'm going to be arrested :(" pretty much just wanting to brag about what was happening.

The cop came over to my window and I told him what had happened with us fighting over the music, leaving out the part that we were on a deadly amount of cocaine. I'm not sure why the cop didn't breathalyze me—maybe because it was 8:00 a.m.—but looking back at this selfie, it was painfully clear I had been tweaking on drugs and under the influence.

I gave the cop my (expired) car insurance and exchanged information with the elderly lady. When he realized my insurance was expired, he wrote me a ticket to appear in court and I was sent on my way. I instantly wished I had listened to my dad, who kept nagging me that I could not drive without insurance, but I'd had higher priorities at the time than paying car insurance. Like buying drugs.

I somehow kept escaping jail, but looking back, I probably needed jail to get my act together. I was furious at what had happened, and it was all my fault, but I kept blaming everyone else in my head. If only Jasmine hadn't begged me to come out that night, I wouldn't have wrecked my car or gotten in trouble.

After crashing at Jasmine's for a few hours, I drove my car home without a front bumper and crawled into bed, where I stayed all day and regretted my choices. The damage to my car was going to cost me thousands of dollars, and I couldn't imagine what would happen when I went to court. That's when I realized the date for my court case was when I was already going to be in California. I called the courthouse to explain to them, but they didn't care.

I finally got the energy to crawl out of bed late that Sunday night and start packing for California. I had to leave early the next morning and I was more than ready to get the hell out of Pensacola. I ended up skipping my court date and having my license taken away for a year with very hefty fines. To this day I am still paying for my stupid decision to drive that night because my car insurance is through-the-roof expensive from having a driving-without-insurance charge on my record.

Ultimately, just like when I ran from Michigan to start over, I was running away again. I thought if I could just start over and have a new life, things would be better and I would somehow be happier. It took me many years to realize that running away doesn't solve the problem when the problem is yourself.

Los Scandalous

L EAVING PENSACOLA WITH A one-way ticket was bittersweet. I wasn't sure when I would fly back, but I assured my friends and my work that I would only be gone a couple of weeks. I figured once my bookings slowed down, I would fly back to Florida and repeat this process every month or so.

When I landed in Los Angeles, I was supposed to call Willer, one of my agency's drivers. I was told that he would be taking me to get tested and then to the modeling house I would be staying at. I wasn't sure what to expect, but since I was with an actual talent agency, I imagined a black SUV picking me up. Someone holding my door for me and treating me like I was important. As for the modeling house, I imagined it would be something like the reality show *Bad*

Girls Club. I pictured a big fancy mansion with a bunch of crazy girls all living together.

I couldn't have been more wrong.

I called Willer and a man with a British accent told me he would be pulling up in a navy-blue Tahoe in a few minutes. Of course he drove the same vehicle as Ryan. That should've been a sign right there. When he pulled up, he put my suitcase in the back for me and didn't pay me much attention. I hopped into the back seat, and then he told me to get in the front, and so of course I listened.

It only took a few minutes before I could tell this guy was a douchebag. He bragged about how good of a music producer he was while I silently thought, "If that was true, you wouldn't be a driver." The icing on the cake came when he said he would only stop at a gas station for me if I gave him oral sex. So not only was I annoyed, I was also sexually harassed.

We pulled up at Cutting Edge Testing so I could go get tested for STDs. As a porn performer, you must get blood and urine tests done every fourteen days. You cannot shoot a scene if you do not have a current clean test. This makes certain that no STDs are passed around. The only way disease is brought into the industry is by performers having unprotected sex in their personal life between their tests.

This is the reason that escorting—which is a nice way of saying being a hooker—is looked down upon by porn producers and some performers. If you are known to have irresponsible sex outside of the industry, you will even be blacklisted by some companies. The porn industry works very hard to be safe and clean, and for the most part it is.

Getting my blood drawn has always made me nauseated, which people always think is ironic due to my body being covered in tattoos that were put there by needles. However, in my mind, they are two completely different things. Another thing: getting tested costs $150 each time—meaning $300 per month. Although it's expensive, you always make your money back (plus plenty) once you shoot your scenes for those weeks.

One of the biggest misconceptions about the industry is that the performers must be "dirty." However, if you are a current porn performer, it is impossible to have an STD if you are shooting. Ironically, these comments usually come from uneducated members of society who themselves haven't been tested in years. In truth, porn performers are far cleaner than your average American.

After my test, Willer was supposed to take me to where I would be staying. Instead, he said he had to drop off some checks with another driver headed to the California Modeling Agency office. We pulled up to the outside of a bar and a skinny drunk guy came running up to my side of the vehicle, clearly very intoxicated. Willer handed me the checks to pass out the window to him.

"You should put these up your ass," he said, slurring his speech.

And that's how I met my future boyfriend, Chad.

Chad was in his mid-twenties but already balding and definitely not blessed in the looks department, but we did share one important bond: drugs. As we drove away from Chad, Willer warned me not to hook up with him. If there was one thing Willer ever said that I should've listened to, well, it was that. He told me that Chad had sex with all of the new porn performers, and that he took advantage of them. Also, apparently Chad had a huge problem with GHB, the date-rape drug. At first I thought Willer was telling me that he would drug the girls, but it turned out that Chad liked to date-rape himself. If you ever want to see someone at rock bottom, observe someone who takes GHB for "fun."

I was a bit shocked by the drivers at my new agency. So much for my vision of fancy, upscale chauffeurs—or even men with manners. I was slowly but surely learning the porn industry isn't as glamorous as people make it out to be. This really sunk in once I saw the "modeling house" I would be staying at.

I walked my suitcase to the door of the model house and a man named Patrick answered the door. Patrick looked to be around fifty years old and struck me right away as a creep. The house was decent, but not what I expected the house to look like. I also expected other models to be staying at the model house—but, nope. It was just going to be me and creepy Patrick. He walked me to the bedroom I would be staying in, and I was shocked to see an empty room with just two twin beds inside, one on each side of the room. No TV, no decorations, no dressers. Just two beds.

I was trying to stay positive. Being in LA, officially starting my porn career with a real agency—these things were exciting, but I couldn't help feeling disappointed. What was I supposed to do without a TV or computer or other girls to hang out with? That all became the least of my worries once I saw how creepy Patrick actually was.

He would barge into my room unannounced while I was lying in bed or not wearing clothes and start telling stories about his ex-girlfriends or whatever other sexual stories he wanted to tell me. One morning he came into the bathroom while I was in the middle of showering to ask me to hold his gun for him because he thought I would "look sexy holding it."

But the creepiest thing he ever did was loudly jerk off to the only porn video of me on the Internet. I could hear my porno very clear from the next room with the added soundtrack of him moaning along. That's when I started locking my door at night.

Thankfully, another girl named Roxanne moved into the house a couple days after my arrival, but things were still very weird. I also met some people in my agency who I hung out with every few nights, so I was gone a lot of the time, and once I finally started booking work, I was too busy and tired to think much about Patrick anyway.

Before you can get booked for any work in the adult industry, most reputable agencies will have you do two things: a photo shoot and some go-sees. The photo shoot is for your agency pictures, and every porn company books girls off of the agency website. Easy enough. New girls are constantly coming in and out of the business, and if a director is looking for new girls, he will scroll through the website until he finds someone he likes. Along with the girl's photos is a list of things she is willing to perform on camera.

When you sign with an agency, they give you a long list of sexual acts and you have to put a checkmark by the things you will do on camera.

Here was my list as a new girl in the business:

Available For:

Anal ☒
Blowjob ☑
Orgy ☑
Boy / Girl ☑
Boy / Girl / Girl ☑
Boy / Boy / Girl ☑
Creampie—Vag ☒
Creampie—Anal ☒
Double Anal ☒
ATM ☒
Feature Dancing ☑

Flexible ☑
Girl/Girl ☑
Girl/Girl Interracial ☑
Interracial ☑
Softcore ☑
Solo ☑
Solo with Toys ☑
Big Toys ☑
Squirts ☒
Deep Throat ☑
Double Vag ☑
Fetish ☑
Bondage ☑
Light Bondage ☑
Girl/Girl/Anal ☒
Smokes Cigarettes ☑
Pegging ☑
Swallows ☑
Foot Jobs ☑
Hand Jobs ☑
Blow Jobs ☑
Load Dumping ☒
Blow Bangs ☑
Bukkake ☒

❖❖❖

BY THE TIME I signed with my third agency, I was checking every single box. Nothing was off-limits for me. Even from the beginning I wasn't opposed to anything on the list, but my agent advised me that saving my first anal scene until I established a name for myself was wiser than just doing them when I was a nobody. If a girl is successful in the business for a couple years, fans will be dying to see her finally take a dick in the butt and companies will be willing to pay double or triple the amount they would be willing to pay otherwise, so I decided to take my agent's advice and shoot vanilla scenes for my first couple of years.

With my agency pictures done, the next thing I had to do were my go-sees. A go-see is when you go with the other new girls to a different company's office so they can see what you look like in person. Kind of like a modeling go-see, except naked. It's pretty much, "Hey, what's your name? Okay, take off your clothes," and you stand there while they stare at you for a bit. This happens at five or ten different companies and then you wait to hear if you got any bookings. Mostly, it's a good way for new girls to be seen and heard about.

I've never had an issue with being nude, but it is a little intimidating when you drop your dress for people to judge if your body is good enough for their movies. The career as a whole is very ballsy. Think about celebrities being judged by their beach bodies and how hard that is for them. For porn stars, our ENTIRE bodies are put under a microscope for men to leave whatever comments they want on videos and forums talking about what they like or dislike about us. We get videotaped in many unflattering angles while having sex. My butthole is plastered all over the Internet for the rest of my life. I have no shame in this matter, but sometimes I don't think people realize how much guts it takes to put yourself out there like that. I think it's admirable.

The same thing goes with being a stripper. You get up on a stage in front of a bunch of strangers in a big room, everyone is staring at you, and then you have to dance and attempt to be sexy in front of them. It can be nerve-racking, but it's something you get used to.

The morning after go-sees, I got a call from my agent. Christy Mack couldn't make it to her shoot that morning, so they asked to have me as her replacement. When I found out the shoot was for Penthouse, I couldn't say "yes" fast enough.

This was my first shoot; I had shot two scenes for Burning Angel, but this was different. I was now part of an adult talent agency and working for any company that wanted me. I was expected to come prepared with everything I could need.

A "porn suitcase" is something every porn star is familiar with. To every scene we get booked for, we have to lug around a giant bag full of many items. Endless amounts of matching bra-and-panty sets, lingerie, bikinis, outfits, shoes, and jewelry. You must bring different options of everything for the director to choose from. Some companies will provide wardrobe, but nearly every time you will wear something you packed in your porn bag. You also want to have a good hygiene kit with you. I always bring lotion, perfume, deodorant, sponges, body oil, tea tree oil, body wash, hydrogen peroxide, iodine, toothpaste, toothbrush, mouthwash, baby wipes, feminine wipes, arnica tablets, extra makeup, makeup remover, and a douche. For an anal scene, the bag also includes an enema, Imodium, and butt plugs.

Prior to my first scene, I had no idea how to use a douche. I had some in my suitcase because I heard other girls talking about them, and thankfully Roxanne was at the modeling house to teach me. She told me to insert the top part into my vagina and then squeeze the bottom so that all of the water went inside of me. I didn't know to make sure I pushed all of the water back out after, and as soon as I sat down inside the driver's car, a gush of douche water came spilling out of my vagina and soaked through my jeans and the passenger's seat.

I was so humiliated, walking into my first scene for a big company like Penthouse looking like I peed my pants.

Thankfully it was the winter and I had a hoodie with me that I tied around my waist. Even with the hoodie, I couldn't escape the embarrassment. When I got up from the makeup chair, the stylist asked me why the fabric seat was soaked. I had to explain in front of a room full of people that I didn't push all of the douche water out of my vagina.

I would get a lot more practice getting all of the water out of me, as I would be doing this hundreds of more times throughout my adult career. It's a bad habit, but it's also something that all porn stars do. Vaginas clean themselves and douching can lead to infections and other problems, but it's considered a common courtesy to the talent you are working with.

There are a lot of weird things that porn stars do on set. For instance, when you are on your period you still have to work, so you shove a makeup sponge up your vagina to stop the bleeding. Within a few months of working in the industry, it became second nature to me, and I can't even tell you how many times a sponge has been stuck inside of me too far to grab with my fingers. Male talent, and even the directors, have helped fish them out after a scene, but sometimes after an hour of hardcore sex it just isn't possible, and it's off to see good ol' Dr. Riggs, who almost everyone in the adult industry went to for all their porn problems. He was experienced all with the common issues in our field. It was common knowledge to go see him if something went wrong. Yeast infection? Go to Riggs. Chlamydia? Go to Riggs. Flu? Might as well just keep going to Riggs.

Porn was a whole new world, but I felt strangely at home. I had never felt more accepted for who I was than when I joined the industry. I felt like I finally belonged. I had always been an outgoing, sexual being who loved attention, so it was the perfect job for me.

My agency had a party and of course everyone that was a part of the agency was invited. I don't remember what the party was for, and the night was a blur. I remember eating a girl out in the bathroom and sucking a random guy's dick behind a dumpster, but everything after that is completely blacked out.

When I opened my eyes the next morning, I had no idea where I was. I was in a bedroom that I had never seen before and there was no one else in the room with me. I wasn't sure what to do, but I was so hungover that I just wanted to go back to the modeling house—and that was saying something.

I heard laughter outside the bedroom, so I decided to go take a look at who the mystery person I had slept with was. I opened the door and see an overweight man that must have been in his forties. My heart dropped. I didn't have high standards, but this was a new low—even for me.

To my relief, I then saw a familiar face. It was Chad, the California Models driver. Chad wasn't a looker himself, but compared to the fat older man, he was the better choice. The older man was his roommate, Eric, with whom I would eventually become roommates too—but I'm getting ahead of myself.

I knew I'd had sex since I woke up completely naked, but I couldn't remember doing it. I didn't tell Chad that, though. I had him bring me back to the modeling house, where I spent the rest of the day sick to my stomach and throwing up from how hard I'd partied the night before.

Chad started texting me the next day and we began to form a friends-with-benefits type of relationship. He would pick me up after work—he was my driver, after all—and we would go to his house. We partied together every few days and did endless amounts of cocaine.

Although I wasn't a fan of his looks, there was something about his personality I liked. He was an asshole, something

I was always attracted too, but he was also funny in his own way. I was attracted to the fact that he was a game. I knew he didn't want a girlfriend and it made me want to see if he would fall for me. I had just started my career as a porn star and was in no position to want a boyfriend either, but I still couldn't help forming feelings for him.

I shot a dozen more scenes in Los Angeles before I decided to make a Miami trip; California Models had agents in both LA and Miami, so I wanted to try them both out before deciding where I was going to live. I knew I would eventually come back to Los Angeles, so I hid the rest of my cocaine under one of the mattresses in the model house. Sure, I was living dangerously, but I had enough common sense to not take cocaine on an airplane.

I had no idea what to expect in Miami, but I was looking forward to shooting more porn. I wasn't scared of my scenes being on the Internet for everyone to see—it was quite the opposite, in fact. I wanted everyone to see them. I was proud of my work and liked what I was doing. I would even post pictures from the pretty girls on my personal social media accounts, usually with the caption being the site you could find the scene on. I craved the attention. I was proud.

I got off the plane in Miami and couldn't wait to see what adventures I'd get myself into the next week. I had a couple scenes booked, but my agent assured me I would get more once I was actually in town.

When my agent found me at the airport, he was with another "porn star"—if you could call any of the Miami girls that. Let's just call them porn girls. They didn't deserve the star title. And this isn't me hating on Miami, but if you are in the industry, you understand.

I learned many girls from Miami go to LA with big hopes and dreams, only to get shot by amateur sites for a week and then no one ever shoots them again. Most Miami girls are young, dumb, and never make a name for themselves. When I found this out, it made me wonder what the hell I was doing bringing myself to Miami when I was already in LA.

The girl my agent brought to the airport definitely did not resemble anyone you would expect to do porn. She was average-looking and wore old, raggedy clothing. It looked like she hadn't showered in a few days and she wasn't wearing any makeup.

When I was brought to the modeling house, I realized this whole "modeling house" shit was a joke. It was the agent's two-story apartment, and he lived with anywhere from six to twelve porn girls at a time. Most of the girls were not attractive and not getting any bookings. The agent's name was Garrett and he made the girls webcam in his bedroom to pay him rent, $250 per week.

If the girls weren't getting booked, not only did they have to webcam, he *forced* them to strip. He would drop them off and pick them up on the weekends so they could pay him rent money. These girls were everything I didn't want to be. They were broke, controlled by Garrett—who was pretty much a pimp—and lived in horrible conditions. While I was living there, six girls shared a bedroom. That's right. They were paying $1,000 each month to sleep in a room with two beds, three girls in each bed.

I was given a side room of the house that wasn't really a room. It was separated from the main room by a curtain and had a small mattress on the floor. I immediately vowed to myself that I would never go to Miami again, and I never did.

A new girl in Los Angeles can easily get $1,000 for a boy/girl scene. In Miami, she'd be lucky to get $600. The whole industry down there had such a different feel than LA. I felt cheap, dirty, and taken advantage of during every shoot.

Out of all the girls there, though, there was one that was unlike the rest, and her name was Jenna Couture. She was a beautiful little petite girl and had such a fun personality. I didn't get to see her very often because she was always working, but when I did, we always connected.

If you're familiar with Jenna today, then you know her as the queen of nastiness—and I mean that in the best kind of way. She is probably the most hardcore chick in porn. However, when I first met her, it was a different story. At the time, she had never had sex with a girl before—I was her first. She also remained very vanilla during her scenes. I taught that girl how to deepthroat like a champ.

I remember one time I was watching a trailer to one of my scenes for a site called Sloppy Girls. In the scene, another girl and I were spitting into each other's mouths and just making a giant mess, slurping and swapping spit back and forth. Jenna was so grossed out, telling me how nasty I was and how she would never do something like that. She actually made me mute the volume. Fast-forward to now, she is drinking pee and shoving butter up her ass and eating it. She has transformed, and I like to think I helped break her out of her shell.

When I would call us sluts, she used to get defensive and tell me she wasn't a slut. I would argue that she had sex for a living and that of course she was a slut, but that it wasn't a bad thing. In fact, it was a good thing! Now Jenna calls herself "The Nastiest Slut in Porn."

I think sluts are given a bad rep. Good for you if you're a girl and go after what you desire sexually. That shouldn't be a bad thing. It's your own body, and you can make your own decisions. I'm all about slut empowerment.

Even though Jenna was more on the softcore side when it came to porn, her personality sure wasn't. She was the biggest partyer I've ever met. I swear that girl was always on molly. I was excited to find a girl who loved drugs just as much as I did.

One day we both had off from work and decided to go to the mall. Before we left her car in the parking lot, she popped three mollies and demanded I take one. I wasn't a huge fan. If it had been cocaine, I would've done it before she had the chance to ask, but molly wasn't fun to me unless I was already fucked up. Sober, it just scared me.

Saying "no" to Jenna was hard. I told her I would take only half of it and then she put the other half in my drink, almost giving me no choice but to take it. I decided to go along with it. We were both in a store's dressing room when it hit me. I yelled over to the next changing room, "Oh my god, Jenna. I'm fucking rolling," and she just about died laughing.

We had so much fun together during my Miami trip that I didn't want it to end. To be honest, I had formed a crush on her. Regardless of whatever type of relationship we formed, I wanted her in my life, so I kept begging Jenna to come to LA to shoot. She wasn't sure about going there and finally confided in me that she was afraid. She admitted that when she and all the Miami porn girls found out I was coming from LA, they were scared too and thought I was going to be some stuck-up California girl, which was hilarious to me.

I texted Chad all about this new hot girl that I met and the first thing he asked me was if we could have a threesome. I wanted to please him, so I told him of course we were going to have a threesome with her. I always wanted to seem like the cool girl he was casually sleeping with that didn't care if he hooked up with other girls. I didn't want to come off like I had any feelings—something I've always done to protect myself.

Since Jenna was already with California Modeling in Miami, it was easy for her to go to Los Angeles, and they immediately set up a flight for Jenna to go to California. She flew out of Miami the week before I did, as I still had a few scenes for Bang Bros I had to shoot. The plan was that she would stay at Patrick's modeling house and once I got there, we could share a room. We couldn't wait to be living together.

Model House Hopping

THE PLAN TO STAY at Patrick's together came to a screeching halt. I hadn't even left Miami when Jenna called me with bad news. When I answered the phone and heard her screaming with someone else in the background. When she finally settled down, she told me that Patrick had kicked her out of the model house.

It just so happened that the bed Jenna chose to sleep in was the same bed that I hid my cocaine under. Patrick was snooping through her things and must've looked under the mattress—which was creepy in the first place—but he found the drugs. Thinking that they were Jenna's, he called California Modeling to have a driver pick her up because she was no longer welcome there.

I was surprised when Jenna didn't rat on me, but it didn't matter anyways. I wasn't going to stay there without her. Though

California Models didn't have any other open model houses, I knew we would figure something out. I felt bad because I was the one who had convinced her to come to Los Angeles, telling her how amazing it would be, and now she didn't even have a place to stay. The California Models driver who picked Jenna up from Patrick's was Chad. When he realized she was the girl I told him about, Chad offered to let her stay at his apartment for free, at least for the meantime.

I told Jenna that Chad was super cool (which I now regret) and that she should stay with him until I got into town. She spent two nights there and was already complaining to our agent that she wanted to live somewhere else.

I guess Chad straight-up told her she had to have sex with him to stay there. Jenna even told me that he went down on her when she told him "no." Once again, I was feeling like I was to blame for making Jenna come on this awful trip.

Thankfully, the day I was getting into town was the day that Jenna left Chad's. So California Modeling had to find a place for us both to stay—and fast. That's when one of the other agents offered to let us stay in his spare room. His name was Connor, and he worked for California Models as the information guy. Basically, he was in charge of texting all the talent what the info for our scene was.

They were supposed to send out all of the information for the scene the day before a shoot, but California Models rarely sent anything besides the time to be there. I'd get a vague text saying something like, "Brazzers shoot tomorrow nine a.m. call time."

When I finally got to a reputable agency, I would see how ridiculous California Models had run things. As a porn star, you need to know if the shoot is providing makeup, what type of clothes/shoes you should pack, if you have any dialogue, who you are working with, etc. I showed up to countless sets with no makeup because California Models didn't tell me to show up makeup-ready. It was embarrassing being represented by people who didn't have their shit together.

Jenna and I were brought to Connor's apartment, where we would stay for the next month and a half. He only had one bedroom, but at most if not all model houses, you had to share the room with another "model" anyway. There was only one bed, though, so we would be sharing that as well.

I didn't mind sharing the room with Jenna. We both loved to party and instantly became inseparable. We were as close as two friends could possibly get. When we both had days off, we'd spend them shopping and doing drugs together. We would also smell each other's vaginas to see if there was any odor and examine each other's buttholes to see if we should bleach or not. We lived together, had sex together, and spent all our time together. We were basically dating, and I definitely formed some major feelings for her.

But the living situation would get awkward after a few weeks. Not between me and Jenna, but between me and Connor. One night I came home from a shoot completely blacked out. I can't even remember how I got home that night, but I woke up the next morning in Connor's bed. I panicked and ran into my own room, where Jenna told me the story.

By the time Jenna came home that night, she walked in on Connor and me having sex—or should I say Connor having sex with me. She said I looked passed out, but Connor insisted I wasn't. I don't have any memory of this taking place, so I'm not really sure what happened that night. Either way, I definitely didn't feel comfortable living there anymore.

Jenna and I were already considering leaving the agency. The main agent had a horrible coke problem, and though I clearly didn't have anything against the use of cocaine, I still didn't want the man running my career to be a druggie. He would always be too hungover or fucked up, and he wouldn't answer his cell phone. Directors always complained that no one was answering the phones in the agency office as well. This was not ideal for the talent.

For example, if I were told by my agent that it was a girl/girl scene and then I got to set and it was a threesome scene with a guy, I would need to call my agent to make sure this is what I was booked for and that I would be getting the appropriate rate for the shoot. When my agent wouldn't answer, I'd be stuck in the awkward situation of not knowing what to do. Sometimes directors will take advantage of new girls, or ones with bad representation, by making them do more than what was agreed on—like throwing extra people into the sex scene and telling you that you also have a solo clip you need to make for them. Directors will get girls to do free scenes all the time if the girls don't know any better, hence we need the correct information the day before the shoot—or for our agent to answer the phone during his work hours. We pay our agents 15 percent of our entire income—the least they can do is their job.

Speaking of money, California Models would book their girls with the lowest rates possible to make nice with directors and I was tired of getting paid less than girls in other agencies. I was serious about my career and I knew I wouldn't get anywhere if I stayed with California Models. I wanted to be represented by an agency that had their shit together.

Jenna had already had several phone calls with an agent at Showcase Models, Victor. She told me Showcase Models was completely different than California Modeling and that we should make the switch.

I was hesitant to leave California Models because I didn't know if this new agency would even be any better. I probably would've waited a few more months to see if things improved if it weren't for Jenna. She was absolutely determined to get the hell out of our agency, and I sat next to her as she called Jackson on speakerphone.

Jenna started the conversation by telling him she wasn't happy and wanted to leave the agency. Of course, Jackson tried to talk her into staying. She was getting booked nearly every single day, making him so much money.

"YOU GUYS DON'T EVEN KNOW HOW TO SPELL MY NAME!" she screamed.

Jackson had no explanation for that one. Jenna Couture was spelled "Jena Coture" on their website. Sure, it might have been a slight mix-up if a director did it, but as her official agent, he needed to have the correct name on his website.

The argument continued to get more and more heated. Finally, Jenna just hung up the phone. She had gotten her point across that she was not happy and leaving the agency. Jenna proceeded to call Victor immediately to let him know she made Jackson aware she was leaving California Models.

I had to make up my mind if I was going to leave with her or not—and quickly. Part of me thought that things at Showcase Models wouldn't be any better than they were at California Models, but I was willing to give it a shot if it meant staying with Jenna. Plus, I didn't want to be left alone with Connor.

Jenna was still on the phone with Victor when I told her to let him know I was going to leave California Modeling as well. He agreed that we could both move into his modeling house the following week. I sent Jackson a text saying that as Jenna's best friend, I was going to follow her decision to leave the agency and that we weren't going to be separated. We would have to finish the rest of the bookings we had for California Models, meaning we had to pay them their commission for those shoots, but then we were free.

We were each to have a meeting with Victor the next day. As soon as I pulled up to the building, I knew this was a completely different agency. While California Modeling was in a tiny strip mall and had a cheap, plain, undecorated one-room office, Showcase Models was located inside the building for Vivid Entertainment, one of the largest porn companies in the world. Vivid owns all of the sex tapes of big celebrities like Kim Kardashian and Farrah Abraham.

The building is beautiful, expensive, and massive. When you walk in, you are immediately greeted by security, which will allow you into the elevator. (Well, maybe not *you*. But as a provocatively dressed porn girl, I was never second-guessed when I said I was there to go to the Showcase Models office.)

As I walked down the long hallways to the office, I grew more and more nervous. This place was the real deal. I pressed the button outside of the office door and was greeted by a woman named Cece, an older British woman who didn't give a single fuck. She always told it like it was, no matter if it was going to hurt your feelings. She was Showcase Models's accountant and kind of like the modeling house mom in that every so often Victor would have her come over the model house to make sure everything was going okay.

The office was so much different than the California Models office I was used to. They had countless magazine covers of their models on the walls in frames, awards everywhere, and giant posters of all of their girls. It looked like their talent had a lot of success. The first time I walked into their offices, I already felt extremely confident with my decision to switch to this agency.

The office was spacious and beautiful. There were at least six different rooms and multiple employees working hard answering the phones, which didn't seem to stop ringing. I finally made my way to Victor's desk.

Victor was complicated. When I first got to know him, he seemed very serious and cold. His voice was entirely monotonous, and he was all business. He had a British accent, a bald head, and icy blue eyes, and he started with very upfront questions—why I wanted to switch agencies, why I wanted to be in the industry, and what I would/wouldn't shoot for him. When the questions were answered, he told me to follow him to the next room, where I was to strip naked.

I took off my clothes while he studied me with a straight face and zero conversation. I turned around so he could see every angle of me naked.

"Very well. Get dressed," he eventually said.

I wasn't sure what to make of his very vague response to my very naked body, but I did as he asked. I assumed he liked what he saw because when we sat back at his desk, he offered me a three-year contract.

When you sign a porn contract, it basically means you have to give them 15 to 20 percent of your income for as long as you sign for. In return, the agent will get you bookings through different companies and directors. You could technically be a "free agent" and book work yourself, but that is difficult for a new girl to start out doing. Agents have all of the contact information for each and every director in the biz. Having an agent is essential to becoming a porn star.

I was nervous to sign such a long contract. I had heard about Victor's reputation for not letting girls out of their contracts, and I had also heard rumors about how if you got on his bad side, well, he wouldn't book you any work and you'd be stuck not working for the remainder of your contract. It pretty much was like signing my career away and trusting him with it for three long years. My gut told me not to, but I had already come this far, so I signed all of the papers and hoped for the best.

When I got back to Connor's apartment, Jenna was there packing up all of her things. I told her how my meeting with Victor went and she told me hers went the exact same way. The only difference, it turns out, was that Victor had made her step on a scale.

I'm not sure why he would have Jenna step on a scale and not me, as I was at least fifteen pounds heavier than her. The only thing we could think of was maybe he wanted her to be tiny to be able to get bookings for "teen" shoots. Although Jenna and I were the exact same age, I wasn't able to get "amateur" or "teen" shoots because I was covered in tattoos. I guess the tattoos took away all my innocence.

It is much harder for a tattooed girl to establish herself in the industry than your average, non-tattooed girl. A non-tattooed girl can be cast as any role in any genre of film. Tattooed girls are only wanted for the "bad girl" roles and tattoo-themed movies, for the most part.

I've never regretted my tattoos, but I did get frustrated at how they stopped me from getting bookings. You would think out of any industry, porn would be the easiest to work in with tattoos, but that is not the case. Some companies won't consider shooting anyone with heavy tattoos.

Although I knew it would be tough, I was not going to give up on my dream of becoming a porn star. And so we finished packing our bags and waited for the Showcase Models driver to pick us up so that we could leave Connor's apartment, and California Modeling, forever.

Porn Star Lifestyle

THE SHOWCASE MODEL HOUSE was known in our agency as the "Front House," as it was located on Front Street, and it was absolutely breathtaking. It was in a beautiful spacious five-bedroom house near Hollywood. I had never lived somewhere so nice in my entire life. The whole place was lined with hardwood floors and the second floor overlooked the gorgeous living room. This was such an upgrade from all of the California Modeling model houses.

This was the kind of life I always wanted to live. Here I was, a small-town girl from Upper Michigan, living in Los Angeles in an expensive mansion, independent, on my own, and doing porn—I was living my dream.

Showcase Models was giving me slightly higher rates than I was previously used to, but I still felt like I was worth more.

For example, I was booked for a live show for Porno Dan, where I was supposed to have sex with three males and two females for $700—which is the definition of bullshit. That wasn't even a proper girl/girl rate. My boy/girl rate was $900, sometimes $1,000, so how was I having sex with three guys for less than that? It made me mad, but I was so happy to be doing scenes at all.

Besides getting less than I deserved moneywise, the rest of my life as a porn star was a living dream for me. My life was sex and drugs. I guess that's what happens when you put six porn stars in a house together.

Jenna and I moved into the open bedroom upstairs. We had to share a room, but it was spacious enough to fit two queen beds, so we didn't mind. We were used to sharing all of our time together, anyway. There were three other girls who lived upstairs with us: Tiffany, Raven, and Holly.

Tiffany was a skinny, bleached-blonde girl who didn't get booked much. She was trashy, with a deep raspy voice she was usually using to complain about something. None of the girls really liked her.

Raven Rockette was a super chill brunette and all-natural girl/girl performer. No one ever had a problem with her. She was always super nice and didn't start any drama. She was the hippie/stoner type.

Then there was Holly, who stayed in the master bedroom, which made sense because she was in her late thirties, *at least*. NOBODY liked Holly. She was skinny but had the most massive pair of fake saggy boobs I'd ever seen. She rarely got booked either, so she spent a lot of her nights stripping at the strip club a few miles away. We always had to hide things from her because we knew she would tattle on us to Victor. Holly was not to be trusted.

There was a bedroom downstairs that another girl named Raven Sky lived in. She was a super skinny brunette Barbie with fake boobs and a fake ass. She always wore fake lashes and the trendiest clothes with the trendiest handbags. She did more "privates" than porn scenes. ("Privates" is what we called prostituting.)

Overall, the house had a fun atmosphere, though. In the morning we would tan naked by the pool, and by midday we'd all be doing shots together. Most of us didn't get booked more than a couple times a week, so we had a lot of free time to do as we pleased.

Jenna and I started to go out to Hollywood almost every night. We were able to get in free everywhere we went. Jenna always got us the VIP treatment because she was fucking most of the club owners. When we went to a club where we didn't know the owner, Jenna would simply give the bathroom attendant a hundred-dollar bill to give us access to a private bathroom all night for us to do coke in. We would break down long fat lines of cocaine on the dirty bathroom floors and snort them up without a care in the world.

The amount of cocaine Jenna and I could do together was unreal. We rinsed out an empty two-ounce face moisturizer container to store our stash in. It was always full of cocaine and we would bring it with us everywhere we went.

One of our favorite pastimes was "coke races." We would make two lines of cocaine as long as we could, sometimes a couple feet long. Then we would each take a straw and get in position. We would designate someone to do the countdown for us and we waited excitedly to get the green light to start our race. Whoever could finish their entire line first was the winner. The money, drugs, and alcohol were endless. As long as we didn't have an early set time the next morning, we would party until the sun came up.

I watched Jenna go to and from privates during the time we lived together, and I grew increasingly curious. The fact that she was sleeping with older men didn't appeal to me, but the large wads of cash she would return with did. Jenna would always tell me if I wanted to make real money, I had to do privates. I was too nervous to go through with it.

I had never done a private before, but technically I had prostituted one time before I got into the porn industry, surprisingly. I had been visiting Michigan one summer when I went to a house party for a local fraternity. The guys all knew I was making a living as a stripper in Florida at the time, so naturally they wanted to see what I was about. I was twerking on the dance floor when a random college kid came up to me and asked if he could pay me to go upstairs with him.

I was always interested in prostituting but never had the balls to go through with it. I remember looking through the Craigslist sex ads when I was eighteen. I don't know why I've been so drawn to selling sex, but it has always been a natural interest. Now that I was wasted and the opportunity presented itself, I decided to go for it.

After giving the random frat boy a flirtatious nod, I followed him up the stairs and into a spare bedroom. He took two hundred-dollar bills out of his pocket and handed them to me. I gave him the sex of his life. I know this because years later he contacted me to tell me he replays that night over and over in his head.

He also confessed to me that he was paying me with the intention of only asking for a lap dance. I was so embarrassed when I learned that he was only offering me two hundred for a dance and that I sucked and fucked him instead. I was an amateur.

Most of the girls in the Front House were constantly going to and from privates, and I decided I was ready to experience that life. The girls all went through an escorting agency connected to Showcase Models, so I knew it'd be easy to get into.

I told Jenna I was ready to do my first private and she put me in touch with the escort agency, which provided me with a date later that night. I was nervous, but I had cocaine to calm my nerves. Lucky for me, I also had cocaine provided to me by my client. I noticed he was smoking something out of a separate baggie, which he later told me was meth. As I was dumping out and snorting lines out of my cocaine baggie, I soon realized that in my fucked-up state I had gotten them mixed up and just snorted a fat line of meth.

I fucked throughout my meth high and left that night with a wad of hundreds and a high. Not just a high from the drugs but a high from the experience. I continued to hook on a semi-regular basis.

The good times would slowly unravel. Jenna and I started having conflicts, as we were with each other nonstop. Living together, sharing a bedroom together, constantly together. We never got a break from each other, and since we were so close, we knew each other's weak spots. When we got into arguments, Jenna would always throw out an insult that she knew would hurt me the most. I threatened to beat her ass after she brought up my eating disorder in an argument. In turn, she called Victor crying that she was afraid I would hurt her.

Victor immediately moved Jenna out of the modeling house and into his house. Victor's house had a couple extra bedrooms that his favorite girls would live in. To be one of his favorite girls, you had to bow down to him and basically worship him. His favorite girls were also the ones that hooked for his escort agency most frequently. I could never be one of those girls. Not because I was against hooking, but because I was against ass-kissing. His favorite girls looked like brainwashed idiots to me. I almost puked every time I heard them refer to him as "Daddy Victor."

Jenna was now Victor's baby, and our friendship would never be the same. We remain friends to this day, but after she moved out of the Front House and into Victor's, we were never quite as close. Also, after Jenna moved out, Victor silently punished me by not booking me for scenes. I knew work had slowed down, but I didn't know it was deliberate by Victor until I got a private message on Twitter from Bang Bros. They told me that they had called Showcase Models to book me but were told I wasn't available. Complete bullshit!

After hearing this from multiple companies, I couldn't stand for it anymore. I sent Victor countless texts telling him I knew what he was doing and that I needed work. I lived in his house and needed money to pay rent.

I obviously wasn't saving any of the previous money I was making because I was spending all my money on dope. It didn't matter if I was staying in or going out. I would do cocaine for breakfast on my desk every morning, then do lines all day long in my room. If I had no one to go out and party with, I would walk to the nearest liquor store, geeked out by myself, and drink myself to sleep with a bottle of vodka.

I was told—not asked—that I had to start web-camming for Victor. He had a room in the office building that was strictly for girls to webcam in. Every girl who didn't get a lot of scenes booked was forced to webcam. It didn't matter if the girl said she didn't want to webcam, he would tell her she could no longer live in his house if she refused, so I knew I wouldn't have a house or a job if I didn't follow his commands.

I would get a text the day before from the agent, V, who was responsible for sending all of the girls their information and schedules. She would tell me what days and times I had to webcam.

There was a soft chair and computer in the office webcam room, and Showcase Models had set up our accounts on their

StreamMate account. This meant they got paid all of the money that I made, and I never saw a dime from all of the endless hours I spent camming in that stupid room.

They would tell me I made less than I did and pocket the rest while putting whatever they claimed I made toward my rent. I started doing cocaine before and during my shows to get through them.

I started hanging out with Jenna less and hanging out with Chad more. Occasionally, all three of us would hang out at the same time. We'd go to bars and both end up having sex with him. I remember the first night that Chad hit me, I rewarded him with a double blowjob with Jenna.

It disgusts me to think that I could still want Chad in my life after he put his hands on me. I remember the exact moment he slapped me across the face for the first time, even through the drunken haze. We were standing in his living room and I told him Jenna and I were going to leave. He demanded I give him my coke before I go. I told him I didn't have any left (a lie) and he slapped me across the face because he knew I was lying. I remember the ringing in my ears from being hit so hard. I instantly broke into tears and Jenna yelled at him. Somehow, we ended up both giving him a blowjob together before leaving that night. That is when Chad knew he could put his hands on me without consequences.

Jenna would tell me I needed to stop associating with Chad and I wish I had listened. Not only because he was abusive, but also because it interfered with my career. Jenna refused to hang out with him anymore, and I wish I had done the same.

Before Chad drove for California Modeling, he was a driver for Showcase Models. Victor had fired him a few years back and they had bad blood. Jenna, being Victor's little angel, knew she couldn't be around someone Victor didn't approve of. Victor knew I was seeing Chad, and that could've also contributed to why he wasn't booking me any work.

I knew things weren't going to get any better for me at Showcase Models if I continued to see Chad, but there was something that drew me to him. Maybe I liked abusive relationships because they made me feel at home.

Chad was trying to convince me to go back to California Modeling, though I wasn't sure they would take me back. I hadn't been happy with California Models in the first place, but it was better than not getting any work at all. The rare scene Victor would book for me was always a weird amateur scene for a guy with a camera and not a legitimate company. When I showed up for a blowjob scene to see an obese dirty man with a camera in his garage alone, that was the last straw. I decided I would try to leave Showcase Models.

There were a few things standing in my way though. One, I had to make sure that California Models would take me back before I left Showcase Models. I didn't want to end up not being part of any agency—then it was certain I wouldn't be making any more scenes. I really wanted to further my career. The second thing stopping me was a big one: I had signed a three-year contract for Showcase Models saying that I would only work for them.

I had heard horror stories about girls having to take Victor to court to try to get out of their contracts. Sometimes Victor would bargain with them, saying that if they paid him $10,000 he would release them. I didn't want to have to do either of these options.

My plan was to give Victor a piece of my mind the next time I left the office after web-camming. In the meantime, I decided to live it up in the Showcase Models house because I knew my days there were numbered.

A porn girl I had never hung out with before texted me asking if I wanted to be in a Riff Raff music video. Of course I wanted to. I Googled Riff Raff to see who he was. He was a white rapper with braids and neon clothing. After watching a few videos of his, I realized he was a ridiculous human being. It didn't matter who it was for, I just wanted to be in the music video.

At the video shoot, I made sure to take selfies with the rapper so I could post them all over my Twitter. From listening to his music before I got to the shoot, I heard him rap about cocaine in some of his songs. I prayed he would have some at the shoot, but everyone was just drinking. The girls I arrived with let me snort some of their molly, but that didn't satisfy me.

I started following the rapper around, telling him he should get a bunch of coke. He seemed like he was all about it but wasn't making moves to actually buy any. To an addict who is craving, waiting is not an option. I started texting my dealer, but he didn't feel comfortable bringing it to a random house where he didn't know anyone. He would bring it to my house, however, so I bailed on the video shoot to get my fix.

I secretly called a taxi and didn't tell anyone I was leaving. When the taxi called me to tell me they were outside, I told everyone it was my agent calling and that I had to take the call outside. I never came back in.

Once liquor was in my system, the urge to do coke grew so large that I could not focus on anything else. If I couldn't get my hands on it or if I ran out, I would drink myself into a blackout because I couldn't handle not being high.

The second the cocaine went up my nostril, I felt instant relief. I instantly calmed down and went into my happy place. All the anxiety and worry vanished. As the cocaine sobered me up, I was finally coherent enough to check my text messages.

KARMEN AMBER VAN DE BUNT

Chad had asked me to go to a club with him that night and I called him, hoping it wasn't too late. He told me to be ready in a half hour—time I used to get higher than a kite. The party was for the industry, an Xbiz nomination party. Nomination parties announced who would be up for the categories on the upcoming awards show.

It's also where people get fucked up and hook up with each other.

I hopped into Chad's truck with nothing but a pint of Smirnoff vodka and my cell phone. I finished the liquor on the way to the club. I wasn't there longer than two minutes before I had a girl up on the bar, eating her out. A crowd formed, of course, and Chad went to go sit down with our agency. There was no containing me as I moved from person to person shoving my tongue down their throats. The best part of porn parties is knowing everyone is down to fuck. You can go up to anyone and it's pretty much guaranteed they will fool around with you.

I saw a familiar face in the crowd: Ron Jeremy. I was new to the industry still and it was the first time I had seen him. Even though he is highly unattractive, I wanted to be able to say I fucked Ron Jeremy. So I did.

I told him how I wanted to suck his cock and he took me to the outside area of the nightclub where people went to smoke cigarettes. Ron told the security guard to watch the back door as I gave him a blowjob and had sex with him. I remember wondering what the hype was about, and that's where my memory ends. I woke up the next morning trying to put the pieces back together of what else had happened and how I'd gotten to Chad's.

He was just as clueless, and thanks to his GHB, he had blacked out along with me.

We checked our cell phones and realized we were the topic of discussion in the industry. Apparently we had sex out in the open at the awards party. Neither of us could believe this, and we thought it was a joke at first until we realized people were very angry. Although our industry is all about fucking, I guess it was looked down upon to actually fuck in the middle of the awards party. Maybe the fact I was fucking an untested agency driver contributed to the taboo as well.

A photo of me completely naked riding Chad's dick in the middle of the club started making the rounds, and, well, that confirmed everything. The ordeal blew over quickly, but it definitely pissed off a lot of people.

No one was as mad as my agent, though. Victor hated Chad and here I was, one of his signed contract girls, having sex with the enemy at an industry get-together. I was already on Victor's bad side for a number of reasons so I hoped he would simply let me leave my contract. From the stories that other girls had told, I expected to have to go to court. I was so fed up with not doing scenes and constantly web-camming for him that I decided to take the risk.

As I left camming in the office, I walked up to Victor's desk to ask why he wasn't booking me. I told him that I knew he was telling people I wasn't available when I was. As I continued to confront Victor, he wouldn't even so much as look up from his computer screen. This made me even more angry.

I had done my research the night before and knew there was no legal way he could bind me into a sexual contract. I spit out some facts that I had read online and stormed out of the office.

Later that day I received an email from Showcase Models releasing me from my contract.

I was free. But I was also about to be homeless.

Dating A Scumbag

NATURALLY, I TEXTED CHAD asking if I could live with him. We were pretty much dating, we just didn't have a title. He was a big factor in my leaving Showcase Models. He hated Victor and reassured me that I could get back with California Models.

Chad happily agreed to let me move into his apartment. I was pretty much already living there anyway. I just needed to move in my belongings, which didn't amount to much. I packed up my two suitcases full of porn clothes, dresses, makeup, and high heels.

I was ready to move out of the beautiful mansion and into a small apartment with two men, and somehow I was excited about this decision. If I could change anything about my time in Los Angeles, I would not have moved in with that loser.

It wasn't hard to get back into California Models. I sent them a bullshit apology email and they agreed to let me back into the agency. I only chose California Models again because Chad worked for them. He was the driver for the agency, and I thought it would be perfect having my boyfriend drive me to and from work. I was wrong. Maybe in any other scenario, but not when the job involves fucking other men.

Looking back, moving into Chad's was a bad decision. For starters, we were not in a solid, committed relationship. Secondly, he had a past of being violent with me—something I should have never put up with. Third, if things went bad between us, I would have nowhere to live.

Now, California Modeling was booking me out a few times a week, which left me with most nights free to be able to party. The shitty rates continued, but it was no use fighting about it anymore.

Chad and I officially called each other boyfriend and girlfriend. Yet he still called me by my porn name. I don't think Chad called me "Amber" even once. That should have been a pretty good indication of how things were going to go.

We had a monogamous relationship. Yes, people in porn consider themselves monogamous. Work is work, but what matters is what happens in your personal life. I'm sure it takes a lot to accept dating a porn star, and I commend anyone who can handle it.

All of Chad's ex-girlfriends were porn stars so I figured he wouldn't have any issues handling it. I was wrong. He'd had a baby with a porn star named Isbabella Grace. I would later learn that Chad was arrested for domestic violence after putting his hands on her. You think I would've gotten my ass the hell out of that relationship, seeing as he had already hit me once before, but I had no common sense at this point of my life.

His other ex-girlfriend was an ex-porn star named Sophia. She was under five feet tall and couldn't have weighed more than ninety pounds. She had the body of a young girl and didn't even look to be of legal age. This innocent-looking blonde girl was the complete opposite of me.

Chad had been fucking Sophia on and off during the summer before we started officially dating in August. They were still good friends and we all hung out in a group on occasion, hitting the bars or the pool together.

Before summer was completely over, we decided to make a trip to Arizona together. It was a tradition Chad did every year with his best friend, Issac. Isaac had a small house out there that we could stay at for free any time we wanted.

Chad, Sophia, Isaac, and I headed to Arizona for a weekend of drugs and partying. Within forty-eight hours, I was locked in the bathroom on the floor crying desperate to go "home."

All four of us had been doing coke since waking up and we spent the morning at the beach drinking. It was getting into the afternoon when Chad and Isaac decided to do molly. Sophia and I were already exhausted and ready to sleep the rest of the day away together. We opted out of the molly party. Chad had been pushing the idea of a threesome on me and Sophia, but neither of us were interested.

Chad had justified it by saying he deserved to have threesomes since I was always fucking other guys for work. Maybe I would have been down for it if it weren't his ex that he wanted to have the threesome with.

In my head, what he was trying to justify was so wrong. I had sex with other people because it was my career and how I earned a living. Chad simply just wanted to have sex with whomever he wanted. I can understand his point of view to an extent, but what I can't understand is what happened next.

Sophia was already lying down in the bed, so I cuddled up and joined her. We had run out of coke, and the comedown was starting to get real. All we wanted was to sleep it off. I was almost asleep when suddenly I heard Chad's voice from right above me.

"Way to go, Karmen," he said.

With those words came a punch to the side of my face. My ears immediately started ringing in pain and I began bawling my eyes out.

What had I possibly done to deserve a punch from my boyfriend? I was minding my own business trying to sleep. The reason he told me later was that he was mad I decided to go to bed because now he wouldn't get his threesome. That was the reason he decided to physically assault me in my sleep.

Sophia started screaming at Chad as I grabbed my phone and locked myself in the bathroom. I had no idea who to call or what to do. I called Jenna, as she was the only other person I had to call. I sobbed through every word trying to tell her what had happened.

Jenna had warned me about Chad, and I wish I had listened to her. This was the second, and surely not the last, time he hit me. She offered to buy me a plane ticket home, but the airport was over an hour away and I had no way of getting there. All four of us had come in Chad's vehicle and obviously he was not going to be kind enough to give me a ride. The only way out was a taxi, but I didn't have enough money for that, so I was forced to wait until everyone went home two days later.

I locked myself in the spare bedroom for the night and well into the next day before Chad even realized I was missing. He knocked on the door and I unlocked it, hoping he was coming to apologize. I had been waiting for hours for this apology, but of course it was not going to happen.

He was high and drunk out of his mind and instantly tried having sex with me. What did I do? I let him. I had no self-worth. I was so angry and hurt by the man whose last interaction was assaulting me, yet I let him into my body. The sex was painful, and he bit down so hard on my lip that it bled. He choked me so hard that I spent most of the sex trying to pry his fingers off my throat.

As soon as he finished, he passed out on the floor.

I went to the kitchen to talk to Isaac about what had happened the night before. He informed me he wasn't going to get in the middle of anything. When Chad woke up later that night, I tried to discuss it with him, but he didn't think he had done anything wrong. He told me I got in the way of his threesome. I couldn't believe this was my boyfriend.

When we got back to Los Angeles, I desperately wanted to break up with Chad, but I was stuck. If I broke up with him, where would I go? I was blowing all of my money on cocaine and didn't have enough saved to get my own apartment. Even if I managed to get an apartment, I didn't have a car or a license. I had no furniture. The only items I owned were two suitcases full of slutty clothes. I started a checklist in my journal of things I needed to accomplish to be able to go off on my own.

First, I needed my license back. It would be expensive in itself, and even if I did get my license back, I wouldn't have a vehicle to drive. It was all very discouraging. People often wonder why women don't just leave abusive relationships— well, this is just one example of why it can be difficult. If I left Chad, I would be homeless. I didn't have any family in Los Angeles to stay with. I didn't even have a car to live in. It would be me and my two pink suitcases on the streets of LA.

I texted the woman who ran the agency's modeling house to see if there were any rooms available to stay in, but there weren't.

I felt hopeless. It was becoming more and more apparent that the only way I was going to be able to afford my own place was if I stopped doing cocaine, so I Googled "Los Angeles cocaine addiction treatment" and found way more results than I could've dreamed of. The problem, however, was that I wanted to get sober and clean in order to save money, and to even step foot in these facilities, you pretty much had to be rich.

I found an outpatient treatment center that would work with my insurance called The Matrix Institute on Addictions in Woodland Hills. That September, I started going three times a week. It was a small treatment center, but I had group and solo meetings that required drug tests once a week, and they provided me with all the tools for sobriety. Chad would drop me off at the Matrix and pick me up three hours later wasted. And as any recovering addict knows, it is just about impossible to recover if you are still associated—let alone living—with another addict.

Most significant others would probably be mindful of their drug and alcohol use around a recovering addict, especially if they were in "love" that person, but not Chad. The freezer was always stocked with vodka; plates of cocaine were always under the bathroom sink. This made relapsing very convenient.

I remember being so fucking proud of myself when I earned my first "Two Weeks Clean" sticker. I took a selfie with that sticker plastered on my cheek and uploaded it to every form of social media, bragging about my accomplishment. Such a small amount of time to the rest of the world, but to me, it was a miracle.

I could get a week or two clean under my belt, but then I couldn't handle the cravings and would relapse. I sometimes would even call my drug dealer to pick me up from treatment early so I could leave and use.

Treatment definitely had its benefits, but sometimes hearing other people's stories and reminiscing about my own was triggering for me. I would romanticize the cocaine use and dream about the burn of snorting my first line. Sitting here right now and putting all this down, I'm four years sober and even writing this is still triggering to me.

From September until December I attended the Matrix Institute, but addiction is a motherfucker. I missed cocaine so much and I thought I could control it this time. By January I was back in full cokehead mode. Chad and I had a routine. We would take shots of vodka, do a couple lines of coke, smoke a cigarette, then repeat. This was a nightly event, and it only ended once the dealer refused to bring more—at which time we would awkwardly lie wide awake in bed, trying to sleep; however, the coke was often mixed with meth, making sleep nearly impossible.

The dope must've made Chad extra paranoid, because he decided to install two cameras in our apartment so he could spy on me. One camera showed the living room and the other the bedroom. He could access the cameras from his cell phone when he was away from the house.

I was constantly being watched, and I never felt comfortable.

Every couple of weeks, my family would receive texts and phone calls from me crying that Chad had hit me again, but they had given up on helping me. I was on a downward spiral and they couldn't do anything.

During one of Chad's violent outbursts, as he attacked me on the kitchen floor, I managed to call my dad, but Chad wrestled the phone out of my hand and hung up. I continued to fight with Chad while my dad panicked from across the country. Since I hopped houses so frequently, he didn't even have my address, so he had to go to the local police station for help.

They contacted the LAPD, who in turn located Chad's place of residence.

When Chad realized my dad had called the cops, he dragged me down the apartment hall, down the apartment stairs, and into the car threatening me in loud whispers. I kept trying to rip away from him as I screamed for help, but no one ever came to my rescue.

I cried hysterically as he drove me around for over an hour. I had no idea if he was going to take me somewhere to kill me, but I figured that was probably my destiny. The police started calling me when they found out I wasn't at the apartment. Chad took my phone away from me and wouldn't let me answer.

Once Chad realized that I would eventually have to speak to the police, he instructed me to call them and tell them everything was fine. Locked inside the vehicle with this monster, I did as I was told. So badly I wanted to yell into the phone "HELP ME" but we were parked up in the hills in an empty dirt lot. I couldn't risk pissing him off.

I had let Chad's violence slide for way too long. Soon I would have the strength to be free from Chad's wrath...but it had almost cost me my life.

911, My Boyfriend Strangled Me!

IT WAS THE MORNING of May 10, 2014, when I saw my life flash before my eyes, but maybe I should start this story from the night before. It was like any other night for Chad and me. We were already drunk, and I had just scored a gram of coke from my dealer. We decided to walk to the local bar we visited frequently to get sufficiently fucked up.

We were laughing and having a great time. Chad was telling his friend how he wanted to get married and have babies with me. This was the same night I was bitching to the same friend privately about Chad's money issues.

When I moved into Chad's apartment, we shared the rent three ways, but once we had his meth-head roommate evicted, we split the rent. Except, really, I was paying the rent in full because Chad had no money.

His excuse was that "I made more money than him," so he found it justified. I found it appalling. I didn't want to be supporting a man—and an abusive man, at that. I bought all of the drugs, all of the alcohol, and paid for everything. I was supporting my abuser. He would threaten to kick me out any time I would refuse to buy him something. I bought him a new cell phone, new clothes, anything he wanted. He had all the power over me.

Anyway, we took the party back to our apartment, and that's when things went from good to horrible. When the cocaine ran out, right on cue, Chad started to get abusive toward me. This was a pattern he established before we even started dating. I expected it each time we snorted our last lines.

He shoved me across the room during an argument, and Chad's friend immediately stepped between us to calm the fire. It ended with the friend putting Chad's drunk ass to sleep in the bedroom and me agreeing to sleep in the other room for the night.

When I was done smoking my last cigarette of the night, I saw Chad's phone sitting on the kitchen counter. I took that and his car keys and locked myself in the spare bedroom with them. I was angry he put his hands on me again and wanted to get him back anyway I could, even if that meant just hiding his phone and keys.

I woke up to the sound of water running. Chad was asleep in the running bath. He must've still been so fucked up that he passed out again. It was around seven in the morning, and I knew Chad had to be at work soon.

I turned off the water and returned to bed, not bothering to wake him up. I was still upset from the night before and didn't care if Chad was late for work or not. Plus, I was so hungover that I didn't want to deal with his bullshit. I bundled my naked body in the sheets and went back to bed.

"Call my fucking phone!"

With those words I felt a kick to my ribs. Chad was standing over me on the bed kicking me awake. I wrapped myself back in the sheets and chose to ignore him. After he ripped the blankets off of me and continued to kick me, I'd had enough.

"Apologize for last night and I'll call your phone," I told him.

A simple request, but not for Chad. Next came the name-calling and wrestling for my cell phone. I tried to run to the bathroom to lock myself inside, but I wasn't fast enough. I kept holding on to my phone with all my might and he tried to pry it out of my hands. Things were already violent, and the last thing I wanted was to be without any form of communication.

The struggle went from Chad trying to get the phone out of my hands to me trying to get Chad's hands off my throat. He couldn't get the phone out of my hands, so he started strangling me. I immediately dropped the phone to pry his fingers off my throat, but he no longer cared about the phone.

The struggle moved from the bathroom to the living room. Whenever I got a gasp of air, I used it to scream "HELP" as loud as I could. I had never been choked so hard in my life, and he wasn't letting up.

My calls for help became quieter and quieter as I now knew I had to save my breath in order to survive. I will never forget the crazed look in his eyes as he yelled, "Die, nigger," repeatedly in my face. Why he chose to use that word, I will never understand.

"You and your dad are niggers," he continued to taunt me.

(Again, my dad and I are both 100-percent white, so I'm not sure why that was the offensive term he decided to use.)

There I was, on the floor while I stared up at my druggie boyfriend screaming "die" as he choked me. I remember thinking, "Wow, this is really how it's going to end. I'm getting murdered right now."

I didn't have much fight left in me, but I wasn't going to give up. Instead of focusing on ripping his fingers off my throat, I tried a new tactic. I dropped all of my body weight to the ground and escaped his grasp.

In that split second, I bolted right out the front door completely naked. To my surprise, the neighbor three apartments down was standing in the hallway motioning for me to come toward her. She had heard my cries for help and was here to save me. I quickly grabbed a doormat to wrap around me and frantically ran into her apartment. She locked us inside her place, where I turned to see her three kids eating their breakfast. I was hyperventilating and could barely talk. She gave me a dress, flip-flops, and a phone to call the police.

I'm not sure where I would've run if my neighbor hadn't been in the hallway, ready to save me. I don't know how my story would've ended, but I am so thankful for that neighbor being there for me.

The police escorted me down to their car to be interviewed and I couldn't stop crying through every word. I couldn't believe I had just fought for my life. I couldn't believe I was sitting in a cop car telling this story. Everything seemed surreal.

As we waited for the other officer to get Chad into custody, my phone started ringing. It was the California Modeling office. I answered the phone in tears, bawling to them about what had happened.

There was silence in return.

"Hello?" I asked into the phone.

"Karmen, where is Chad? He needed to pick up Janice fifteen minutes ago," my agent said, as if I hadn't just told him I was nearly strangled to death.

"Your driver just tried to kill me!"

Still no reaction from my agent. Just a simple, annoyed, "Have him call me if you see him soon."

I knew my agents were shitty people, but I didn't know how big of pieces of shit they were until that moment. Not a single drop of compassion or care for me. That was the least of my worries when the second officer approached the car.

The officer informed us that the apartment was empty and that Chad was nowhere to be found. They asked me for his vehicle information, but I suddenly remembered that I had hid his keys with his phone the night before, which meant Chad had fled on foot.

Knowing he had no keys and no way to get back into the complex, they escorted me back up to my apartment to discuss the details of the assault further. I couldn't believe I had almost been strangled minutes before in that same room.

They took photos of my injuries for proof in court. They took pictures from all angles of the red handprints and marks covering my entire neck. My acrylic nails had ripped off along with my natural nail from trying to pry his fingers off my throat.

I was given an emergency protection order from Chad. This meant he was not allowed to contact me or come within one hundred yards of me or the apartment. This was granted along with an immediate move-out order for Chad, meaning the apartment was mine. All of my worries about not being able to afford a new apartment were gone. Even though Chad's name was on the lease, the move-out order made it mine. The landlord asked if I wanted to switch apartments in the complex to a newer unit, one that didn't have any bad memories, and I happily accepted his offer.

The police recommended that a friend pick me up so I could stay with her for a few days until Chad's belongings were out of the apartment. It was difficult for Chad to get his stuff back when he wasn't allowed on the property nor allowed to contact me. His friend, Isaac, who witnessed his abuse in Arizona, played middleman, coming over every now and then to collect bags of his items. I was happy to see everything go. I didn't want any memories of that scumbag in my home.

I still had more scumbags in my life I had to rid myself of, however: my agents.

I texted and called Jackson well over twenty times that day with no response. The only person who contacted me was Connor, and that was to send me my information for a scene two days after my domestic violence attack. When I replied asking details, I got no response. Nobody would answer my calls.

The scene was for a BDSM site I had shot for in the past, and it had been hard enough to handle then. How would I be able to handle such a rough scene two days after I had almost been strangled to death? I was furious that my agency would book this for me. It showed how little they cared about me.

I went to work and tried to put on a front and do my job, but I broke down crying in the opening scene: me, tied up outside and blindfolded, while Erik Chase shocked me with electricity. We had to cut so I could collect myself and stop sobbing.

When we went back to shooting twenty minutes later, it was time for the sex to start. Erik was fucking me from behind outside on the ground and he was shoving my face into the dirt. As I tried to breathe, I inhaled and choked on dirt and grass. This was when I completely lost it. I was still traumatized from Chad's attack not even forty-eight hours before and here I was letting myself be treated like complete garbage again. I couldn't handle it. I couldn't finish the scene. A thousand dollars wasn't worth the pain this was causing me emotionally.

I was usually good at numbing myself before abusive scenes and taking my mind completely out of it, but I couldn't put on an act today. I was mad at myself for coming to the scene. I was mad at my agents for booking it for me. I felt worthless.

It was time I got all of the negative people out of my life once and for all. When I got home from the shoot, I immediately wrote my last email to California Models. And of course, I never got a response. The only way I even knew they read my email was that eventually they pulled my photos from their website. California Modeling was finally out of my life. Chad was out of my life…well, almost. Our relationship was finally over, but the countless court dates would keep us seeing each other for the next eight months.

Sugar Baby

I WAS AFRAID TO go anywhere after the assault. I worried that Chad would want revenge on me for pressing charges. I was paranoid he was hiding everywhere and that he was going to try to kill me. I was constantly looking over my shoulder, worried that he had hired a hit man, which he had talked about in the past—hiring a hit man on one of his enemies. I wasn't just afraid for a few days or a few months, either. To this day, when I see a truck that looks like his, my heart sinks. When I'm in Los Angeles, I constantly make sure I don't see him in any public place I'm in. This is something that will follow me forever.

As time went on, I decided I needed to go out and celebrate my breakup. I wasn't going to let this douchebag continue to control my life. I was free of him, and it was time to act like it.

There was a guy I knew from before I started dating Chad that really wanted to be my sugar daddy. I knew he would jump at the opportunity to finally hang out with me, so I texted him letting him know I was single.

A few hours later, there was a limo waiting for me outside of my apartment. I snorted coke in the empty limo on the way to his house. I was nervous to finally hang out with him, but Jenna said she would meet us later that night, so I felt more comfortable.

Chad hadn't let me hang out with Jenna during our entire relationship, the reason being that she had talked bad about him in an interview for a website called *The Real Porn WikiLeaks*. She told the truth about how he had sexually assaulted and attempted to drug her and many other models. I had been dating Chad when the interview came out, and I knew every word of it was true. The article was called "What the Hell Is Going On at California Modeling," and it addressed all of the issues with Chad and California Models that I've been telling you about.

I was excited to reunite with Jenna, but also nervous to be hanging out with my sugar daddy. His name was Richard, and I had never been alone with him. I met him through an old friend who used to be his sugar baby.

Richard was probably in his late forties (I thought it would've been rude to ask his age), balding, short, and chubby. He definitely would not have been able to hang out with hot porn stars every weekend unless he was rich.

The reason I chose Richard as my sugar daddy wasn't the money, as most people would assume. I chose Richard because he was the biggest cokehead I knew. He always had a vial of cocaine on him. He would pass it to me constantly in public. Any time I had to go to the bathroom, he knew to give it to me.

The coke never ran out with Richard, not even once. We would do at least five or six grams between the two of us on any given night. Some nights we would be with up to ten other girls and he still had enough to supply us all.

I would invite as many girlfriends as I could to come out with us every weekend. He would buy us all Bebe dresses and supply us with tons of liquor and cocaine before going out. We only arrived at the clubs by limousine, and we always had VIP. It was pretty much a party girl's dream.

Once Jenna and I got our hands on each other after my breakup, we were back to being inseparable. We picked right up where we'd left off. We went out with Richard at least once a week, doing more cocaine than most people would think is humanly possible.

Richard even paid to fly Jasmine into LA from Pensacola. I hadn't seen Jasmine in a couple of years and was so thankful to him for the chance to see her again. He provided us with all the party supplies we needed, and we had a wild weekend on him.

Richard's favorite thing to do was get fucked up and take me shopping, which I loved as well. Makeup, lingerie, dresses—you name it, he bought it. Along with the endless supply of drugs, alcohol, and shopping, he would give me five hundred dollars the morning after, before his driver took me home.

I was living the life. I mean, of course I had to sleep with the guy, but I was always blacked out when it happened, so I never really remembered it anyway. It was an easy transaction and I was used to using my body to get the things I wanted.

The only bad part was that Richard had started to fall in love with me. I had just broken up with Chad, and the last thing I wanted was any sort of commitment—especially with my sugar daddy.

The idea of marrying a rich old man sounds like a fantasy to most whores, but I always felt a different calling. I knew that one day I wanted to eventually live a normal life with a husband I actually loved and have kids.

I played along and acted like I had feelings for Richard too, but that was only so I could keep getting beaucoup free coke. Soon, things would come to an end and Richard would never want to hear from me again.

There is only so much dope a person can snort before they reach a breaking point.

The Mental Breakdown

I WAS ON MY way home after a two-day bender with Richard. It was ten in the morning, and I hadn't slept in over forty-eight hours. I had so many drugs in my system that I felt like I was already halfway to death.

I put on a smile while Richard brought me home and he planned on seeing me later that night, but I knew I couldn't handle another night of partying. I just felt off.

When I got up to my apartment, I was still coming down from all of the cocaine. This particular day, the ride back down was more intense than others. I think I might have been snorting a lot of coke cut with meth that night.

My memory of the day is a bit hazy, but after talking to Jasmine and my sisters about it, a lot has come back after all these years. The part I can vividly remember is of me lying in bed and hearing voices— and the voices were telling me to kill myself.

I was trying to close my eyes and fall asleep, but with all of the drugs in my system, my brain was fighting it. I felt absolutely psychotic as I tried to drown out the voices with the volume of the TV, but the noise was overwhelming. I burst into tears and couldn't stop bawling. The voices were driving me literally insane, and I couldn't stop them. I was so tired but so doped up on uppers that I wasn't sure if I would ever be able to fall asleep again.

I didn't know what to do. I started calling my sisters. I knew they were hanging out together that day after seeing them together on Snapchat, so I figured I would call them to say goodbye.

"I'm going to jump off my balcony," I said between sobs.

My sisters were visibly annoyed. They told me they were busy visiting animals at the humane society and that they couldn't talk. You know you're a complete train wreck when talk of suicide doesn't make your family flinch anymore. I could hear them talking to each other, irritated by my statement. They knew I was a cokehead and that I was on a bunch of drugs. They didn't feel sorry for me in the least, and I didn't blame them. They hung up on me.

This sparked my depression to grow even greater— something I didn't even think I could achieve at that point. Next, I decided to call Jasmine. She was supposed to come visit me in a few days, but I didn't even want to live until then.

Jasmine's response was more compassionate. I'm sure she was just as irritated, as she had heard me say this type of thing a number of times over the past four years, but she didn't let me know she was annoyed if she was. She asked where I was and if I was with anyone.

I was so sick from coming off all of the coke that I couldn't stand to talk anymore. My head had so many noises in it, and

I didn't want to speak. I hung up on Jasmine and put my phone on silent.

Jasmine, not being able to get ahold of me after my suicide threat, went into panic mode. She called Richard to come check on me, and I had no idea. When Richard knocked on my apartment door, I was FURIOUS.

I never told Richard my apartment number, so I knew Jasmine had spoken to him. I didn't want him to know which apartment was mine. I always had the limos and drivers pick me up in front of the complex. I didn't feel safe with Richard knowing my apartment number in case he ended up being crazy.

I refused to answer the door for Richard and texted Jasmine, bitching her out for telling Richard. Now Richard knew I was mentally unstable, and it took away the sex appeal of our relationship. I figured she had ruined my relationship with Richard by telling him I wanted to kill myself.

Of course, Jasmine was just looking out for my safety and doing whatever she needed to keep me alive, but through the haze of drug withdrawal, all I felt was attacked and betrayed by my best friend.

I told Richard he was a fat cokehead that had to pay for pussy. I told Jasmine she was a fat stripper with no tits and that she was the "less hot version of me."

(Yes, I quoted *Mean Girls* in a serious argument.)

I burned two bridges and I couldn't take the words I had said back.

By the time I got done fighting with everyone, my mood went from suicidal to homesick, and I thought that if I could just get back to Michigan, everything would be okay. If I could just go home, I would go back to being happy and safe.

I booked a flight for the next day and called my dad, crying that I needed to come home.

KARMEN AMBER VAN DE BUNT

Long coke binges usually resulted in me crying that I needed to go home.

Jasmine would still come to LA a few days later, even though I wasn't in town. She stayed with Richard and I'm sure they had a wonderful weekend of talking shit about my crazy ass. I was so upset that they were hanging out together when they both only knew each other from me. She was stealing my sugar daddy.

I got to Michigan with the intention of starting my sobriety—again. This time I felt ready. I didn't want to experience a comedown like that ever again. I'd felt completely out of control and like a "real" drug addict.

I would be clean of cocaine for the next four weeks. Not by choice, but because cocaine wasn't available in Upper Michigan—at least not anywhere I knew about. Instead, I would binge-drink every night.

Each morning I would feel remorse and disappointment with myself for drinking, but the cycle continued the entire month that I was home.

The moment that alcohol touched my lips, I would get such a strong craving for cocaine, but there was no way of getting it. Instead I just drank until I couldn't walk anymore. I found the occasional pill to snort to replicate the burn of cocaine in my nostrils, but it wasn't the same.

By the end of my trip in Michigan, I was ready to go back to Los Angeles. I needed my fix.

Meeting Alex

I LANDED IN LA late that Saturday night and all I wanted to do was sleep. However, when I got a Twitter message asking me to come party, the thought of using cocaine overpowered my need for sleep. It had been a month since I had done cocaine, though it felt more like a year to me.

I had never met the guy who invited me out, but when I checked out his Twitter page, he seemed legit. He worked at a nightclub so I knew I could party and drink for free all night. I was there. I texted my friend Emily to join me so that I didn't have to show up alone.

Emily was a tall blonde who worked in the porn industry as well. I hit her up because she was just as addicted to cocaine as me. I knew that if I offered to share my coke with her, she would join me, no questions asked.

The guy on Twitter sent me his address so we could pregame at his apartment before heading to the nightclub. Emily and I had already been pregaming at my apartment, but we weren't about to turn down free booze and possibly more drugs.

In the elevator at Twitter guy's apartment complex, we finally reached his floor. The guy said that he and his two friends would be waiting for us to walk us to his apartment. As the door opened, I instantly locked eyes with this gorgeous man standing there waiting for me. I didn't even get a chance to look at the other two men because my focus was all on Alex.

I confidently walked right toward him, shaking his hand and introducing myself. Alex was tall, dark, and handsome. He was six foot three with muscles like I had never seen before. He was a light-skinned black man, my personal preference, and I was instantly drawn to him. His outfit was flawlessly put together and his hair was perfectly styled in place.

Alex followed me around the nightclub all night, trying to dance and talk to me. All of his attention was on me, and I knew we were going to have sex.

When we left the club, Alex didn't come with us, so I ended up giving two of his friends head in the Uber back to Twitter guy's apartment. When I got there, I ended up having sex with one of them.

While outside smoking a cigarette after, I saw Alex walking toward me. I was so happy he had come back to find me. We didn't have each other's phone numbers yet, so he'd just hoped I would be there—though I'm sure he hadn't hoped I had already hooked up with his friends.

Alex and I immediately started having sex outside the apartment complex. We were trying to make our way to his car but stopped to have sex on a random car on the way there. Eventually we made our way to my apartment complex to finish what we started.

Waking up the next morning, I could remember bits and pieces of the wild sex we'd had in my bedroom the night before. I'd had one-night stands with many men, but Alex was different.

He didn't rush to go home as soon as he woke up. Instead we lay in bed and got to know each other for a couple hours. I made up a fake appointment I had at noon so he would leave. I didn't like getting to know men. I didn't want to get attached and get my feelings hurt.

I found out that Alex had actually been working at the night-club the night before. He got paid to drink and flirt with girls all night. Oh my God. I fucked a promoter. I had always been turned off by slimy club promotors, though Alex didn't fit the stereotype.

We exchanged numbers and full names before I ended up kicking him out of my place. I wasn't planning on anything serious happening, but I figured we would probably have sex a few more times. Or at the very least I could hit him up for free tables at the club.

Immediately after Alex left my apartment, I began stalking his social media. I came across his Twitter, and his profile picture featured him kissing another girl. After thoroughly stalking him, it looked like he was in a long-term relationship with a girl who was my complete opposite.

This girl was conservative, preppy, and gave off such a fancy, stuck-up vibe. I was tattooed, slutty, wild, and free. I wondered what the hell Alex was doing chasing after a girl like me all night.

I ended up letting Alex come back to my place later that night, and I asked him if he had a girlfriend. He didn't and claimed he just hadn't used his Twitter in a long time. Either way, I didn't care too much; he was only a hookup to me.

Or so I thought. By our second morning together, I could tell there would be something more between us. He was actually far from the dominant man he'd portrayed himself as on the first night.

In fact, Alex is probably the only gentleman I've ever met my entire life. He is a man who had truly been raised the right way. He is the most respectful, kind, and genuine man there could ever be. His needs were secondary to mine from the get-go.

I was used to guys treating me like shit my entire life. I was intrigued by someone who thought I was worth something more than sex. Alex also called me "Amber," which didn't even feel like my name anymore.

Everyone in Los Angeles only knew me as "Karmen" because that is what I'd gone by every day for work. None of my porn friends called me by my real name. Chad had always called me Karmen. Karmen was even the name I gave the baristas at Starbucks. I had completely forgotten that "Amber" existed.

Alex stated that I've always been "Amber" to him and that he saw through the "Karmen" facade. It felt nice to hear my real name every once in a while.

Although things started moving fast between us, I didn't think we were going to be long-term boyfriend/girlfriend. For starters, I was a porn star. No one would want to marry a porn star. I knew I wanted to be married one day, but it definitely wasn't in my near future. On top of that, he had just gotten out of a three-year relationship a few months prior, while I had just ended my abusive relationship with Chad two months before.

As they say, things happen when you don't expect them to. We became obsessed with each other. We were saying "I love you" a little over a month later, and Alex moved into my apartment just as soon.

Court Battles

IT WAS THREE MONTHS after the domestic violence with Chad had happened. He hid from the police each time they came knocking, and I wasn't sure if he would even show up to court.

Alex insisted on accompanying me to the court case. I was so scared to be in the same room as Chad again and I felt much safer with Alex there to protect me. Alex was shocked when he saw what Chad looked like. He had imagined some big, intimidating guy. Instead he looked at the five-foot-six, 140-pound coward and laughed.

I would've loved to have read Chad's mind when he saw my upgrade of a boyfriend.

The state was pressing charges against Chad for the domestic violence whether I wanted to press them or not.

He pled guilty. There was too much evidence for him not to, between the photos of handprints on my neck and the neighbor who was a witness. Plus, this was the second domestic violence trial against him. He had been in this same position just years before with his own ex, and he knew that if he went to trial, his chances of winning were slim to none.

Chad took a plea deal and got to choose between two weeks in jail and 240 hours of community service, along with court-mandated domestic violence classes and regular court check-ins. What I was happiest about was the three-year restraining order the judge issued in my protection. I felt safer knowing he legally wasn't allowed to contact me or come near me.

Although I knew he deserved much more time, I felt content knowing he was punished for what had happened. I cried tears of happiness as Alex and I left that courtroom. I felt such relief believing that was the last time I ever had to see Chad's face again.

But, of course, it didn't end that easily.

Just when I thought things were done with Chad, it turned out they had just begun. I was on set for Penthouse, sitting in hair and makeup, when an "Amazon delivery man" walked into the room.

He handed me a stack of papers and said, "Amber Teliin, you've been served."

Chad had hired a man to show up on my set dressed as a deliveryman to serve me. The male talent I was working with that day was from California Modeling, and I knew that Jackson must have told Chad I would be on this set today. Being that Chad drove for California Models, he knew gate codes to get onto certain house locations.

Not only was it completely humiliating to be served papers at work, it made me look terrible in front of the director. I flipped through the paperwork, trying to figure out what was going on.

Chad filed for a restraining order against *me*.

I was livid but found the whole thing humorous at the same time. I had not talked to Chad since the morning of the assault. I wanted nothing to do with him and was moving on with my life. I couldn't wait to see what he was going to come up with in court. I knew that it was going to be a long, petty road to get rid of Chad.

I didn't hire a lawyer because I knew Chad had absolutely no case against me. I was fairly confident when I came to court this second time.

After going through security, I stopped in the bathroom to freshen up before it was time for our case. While going through my purse to find my hairbrush, I found a small baggie of coke.

My heart sank. I instantly ran to the stall and flushed the evidence of drugs down the toilet. This was the same purse I had just gone through security with.

If they had seen the blow, I could have been charged with possession of cocaine...at court! That charge could have carried up to five years in prison and a felony. Worse, if I had been caught, Chad would have gotten all the gratification he could have ever hoped for! I couldn't believe I had unknowingly snuck coke into the courthouse. I just felt so lucky I was the one discovering the cocaine and not a police officer.

The trial went just as I had expected. The judge asked Chad when the last time that I had spoken to him was, and he said, "May tenth." It was now September. When it was my turn to talk, I explained to the judge that I wanted nothing to do with him and that this was retaliation for the domestic violence charge. Luckily, the judge saw right through Chad's actions.

Her exact words to Chad were, "She has clearly moved on and does not want anything to do with you." That might have been one of the best moments in my life. The case was dismissed.

Sounds like everything is finally over and done with? Not even close. There was no stopping Chad and his court-happy ass.

It was October when I answered a knock at my apartment door. I was served for a second time, and obviously I knew it was from Chad—but for what this time?

I became fully enraged when I realized these were papers saying he was suing me for $5,000. He claimed I had stolen his belongings. Some of his belongings were indeed in my apartment, but not because I wanted them or stole them. Chad wasn't allowed within one hundred feet of me or my apartment, so he was not allowed to come get his belongings himself. He had to hire a mover to do so, which he had not. He was not allowed to communicate with me, so I was stuck with all of his crap for months.

All of his belongings were gross and worthless, but I knew I couldn't throw them away for this exact reason. It wasn't my fault I had his items, and it was his responsibility to get a third party involved to retrieve them.

I decided to hire a lawyer this time. I didn't want to take any chances of having to owe Chad money for the crap I didn't even want in my house. When the lawyer heard my case, he wasn't worried at all. He told me the judge would see right through Chad's bullshit and be able to tell the truth. Plus, I had screenshots from his ex-girlfriend telling me all of the belongings were things that *she* bought that he had stolen from her previously. She even told me she had receipts proving she purchased the items he was suing me for.

When we got to court, Chad had a cocky smirk on his face. Before the trial started, we were told to review each other's evidence in the hallway with our lawyers. Chad was out of his mind. He had prepared a binder of documents that was an inch thick. Flipping through these pages, I couldn't believe my eyes.

Chad had printed out every porn photo of me on social media. Photos of me with my fist in another girl's asshole. I wasn't sure how any of this was relevant to him wanting his belongings back, but this just showed how desperate he was to make me look bad.

He had also named me in the lawsuit as "Amber Teliin aka Karmen Karma," just because he wanted to let the judge know I did porn, hoping to ruin my character.

Chad was continuing his abuse by taking out all these court trials on me. He wanted to keep ruining my life and refused to leave me alone. The judge saw that. I told him I didn't want any of the items he had at my apartment, but we simply were legally not allowed to contact each other. He told Chad to have movers pick up his belongings within the next two weeks or that I was allowed to get rid of them. He dismissed Chad's other charges trying to get me to pay for damage to his old apartment and other fraudulent claims he'd come up with to get back at me.

I could have sued back for the $1,000 of merchandise Chad had of mine in his vehicle or even filed a countersuit for harassment and fraud, but I didn't care about all that. I truly just wanted everything with Chad to be over and done with. I didn't want any money from him. I didn't care about getting my items back. I just wanted him far, far away from me.

When the judge read the verdict, Chad was visibly pissed off. He even yelled at his lawyer for not doing his job right. He left the courtroom and that was the last time I ever saw Chad.

I was thrilled that my nightmare was finally over.

Recovery

SINCE ALEX WORKED IN a nightclub, we were in the club scene a few times a week. Fridays and Saturdays, I would invite all of my porn friends to come to Sound Nightclub with me so we could party for free at a VIP table!

Alex's boss loved that he was dating me because I always brought slutty chicks to dance around. The VIP clients loved that. It kept them coming back and spending their money week after week.

I would be snorting lines off the side of my hand in the middle of the club. If I had acrylic nails that day, I would do nail bumps. I didn't give a fuck who saw me snorting lines. I felt like royalty in the club scene. I got whatever I wanted, did whatever I wanted, and no one said anything.

I would make out with girls, get completely naked, do drugs, eat out my friends—I was out of control. I even ran down Hollywood Boulevard topless. It's a miracle that I have never been charged with indecent exposure or possession of cocaine.

If Alex wasn't working, then we were at one of my friend's houses, bingeing on coke. Alex rarely partook; he would watch me snort the night away and then make sure I got home safe. He would start begging me to go home around two or three in the morning, but we never left before the sun came up. The night usually ended with me twerking in the passenger's seat, rapping to trap music at eight in the morning, high as a kite.

If Alex was mad, I never noticed. I also never cared. Nothing besides the coke supply mattered when I was partying.

The morning after—or, fine, the afternoon after—I would wake up with a wave of immediate guilt. I would lie there with my eyes closed, trying to put together the pieces from the night before. I would pretend I was asleep as long as I could to hide from the shame I would feel when I had to face Alex. He would usually joke about the mean behavior I'd had the night before, but it was very clear it bothered him.

I did things like ignore him all night, run away from him in the clubs, hide in the bathroom doing coke all night, kiss random guys, and so on. And even if I didn't do any of those things, I still felt remorse for my actions. It was embarrassing letting him see how addicted to coke I truly was. I would dial my dealer a hundred times if it took that many tries. If I needed coke, I would stop at nothing to obtain it.

Alex and I had dated for about three months before he confronted me about my addiction. I was a bit defensive but agreed I needed to slow down. We agreed that we would only party once a week from now on: Saturday night.

This plan worked out for a couple weeks, but after a while, I started to talk him into letting me do it twice a week, then three times a week. I couldn't stop.

I would sit home, trying to stay in, but I had nothing else on my mind besides cocaine. We knew it was a problem. Alex had a solution.

Alex was obsessed with weight lifting, which was something I had never tried. Sure, I had been to the gym, but only during my eating disorder days, when I would do hours of cardio. I had never lifted a weight in my life.

Alex had given up his workout sessions in order to spend time with me for the first few months of us dating, and I knew he missed it. He thought it would be a great opportunity to start taking me to the gym with him. It would also be a great distraction from going to the club.

I honestly felt too intimidated to lift weights with Alex. My nerves were so high the first day we planned on going that I snorted two Adderall beforehand. I figured it was a great preworkout for a druggie.

When we pulled up to the gym, my heart was racing so fast that I was having chest pains, and I knew I would be in serious trouble if I raised my heart rate even higher in the gym. We drove home. Once again, I felt ashamed.

When I finally faced my fears and went to the gym with Alex, it wasn't as intimidating as I thought it would be. I was always one of the only girls in the weights area, but I found it empowering.

Alex taught me lifts for every muscle group and I started to love the natural high that working out gave me. I loved the feeling, and I was proud of myself for being productive and doing something nondestructive to my body for once in my life.

Alex and I started to go to the gym on the weekends. He quit his job at Sound Nightclub because he knew it was triggering for me. If either of us went to a nightclub, there was no way I could stick to recovery. He got a new job working at LA Fitness, and it made sticking to my new lifestyle even easier.

Along with recovery, Alex thought it would be healthy for me to rekindle my relationship with my mother. I had told him about all of the horrible things she had done in my life, but he didn't understand the full extent. Perhaps he thought I was exaggerating.

At that point, I was not on speaking terms with her. She had tried to steal $750 from me, so I'd cut her off about six months prior. As shitty as she was, I still yearned for a mother-daughter relationship, and I agreed to give her another chance. This only consisted of the occasional text message every few weeks. She said she was proud of me for working on my sobriety, but I questioned if she really felt that way. My mom was a terrible alcoholic and during my attempts to be sober in the past, she had always encouraged me to drink with her.

This only lasted for about a month before I was disappointed once again. It was Christmas morning of 2014. I opened up the gift my mom had shipped me and was left speechless. It was a bottle of Patron.

Here I was, six weeks sober, face-to-face with a fifth of tequila. Everyone in my family was silent when they saw what I'd opened. My mother, who knew I was a recovering alcoholic, bought me booze for Christmas. That couldn't sum up that evil woman any better.

Dad insisted I throw the bottle away, but I convinced him I was going to take it home for the purpose of giving it to my roommate.

The reality, though, was that I was saving it for myself.

The Planned Relapse

I SECRETLY PLANNED OUT my future relapse. I decided to drink and use again during the duration of the AVN weekend. Adult Video News hosts a four-day event for both performers and fans every January in Vegas. The expo starts on Wednesday and ends Sunday. The performers sign autographs and take photos with fans at assign-ed booths, and it's a great way to make money and meet your fans.

It's also the perfect excuse for day drinking.

Saturday night was the big event: the AVN Awards Show. Performers waited all year for this one day—to show off on the red carpet and to hopefully win a trophy at what everyone calls "The Oscars of Porn."

This weekend was filled with parties for the industry, so I didn't want to miss out on the fun. I would take my bottle of tequila and a ball of cocaine to Vegas to relapse. I told myself it was okay because it was a planned relapse and not a moment of weakness. An addict will find any way to justify using.

I finally shared my plan with Alex, who was not sold on the idea. I told him it would be the last time and that it was my decision. As always, Alex stopped arguing and went along with me. He knew that when it came to my cocaine use, there was no way to reason with me.

He drove me to Vegas on Wednesday night and dropped me off at the Hard Rock Hotel & Casino. I was sharing a room with my roommate, Kim. Alex immediately had to turn around and drive back to Los Angeles. He had to work Thursday and Friday but planned on driving back to Vegas after work on Friday. That's right. He drove back and forth to Vegas twice just for me.

My original plan was to relapse on Friday, but without Alex to be the angel on my shoulder, I relapsed right away Thursday morning. My roommate Kim and I went to the main floor of the Hard Rock to get Starbucks, but then she decided to go into Pink Taco for a shot instead. This was our biggest weekend of the year, and everyone was drinking at all hours of the day.

I told her I wasn't going to drink, but once I sat at the bar, I decided one shot wouldn't hurt since I was going to relapse the following day anyway. One shot turned into five, and I was officially shitfaced by 10:00 a.m.

When we got back to our hotel room, I immediately dug into my stash of cocaine. I snorted lines between doing my hair and makeup for the expo. By the time I was walking down to sign at my booth, I was in full party mode.

I spent all Thursday going back and forth to my hotel room to take shots of tequila from the bottle my mom bought me for Christmas. Thankfully, there was a saltshaker in our room, so it worked out perfectly.

Spilled salt and cocaine residue covered the top of the black dresser in our hotel room. It was the first time I had drunk in a couple of months, so I got fucked up really fast. I have no recollection of being on stage accepting my award for Throated Deepthroat Queen of 2015, but apparently I tried to deepthroat the microphone during my speech. This made the microphone screech, hurting everyone's ears at the event. How embarrassing.

I was supposed to attend a party that my agency was hosting that night, but I was passed out by dinnertime. I had partied way too hard, way too early.

I switched to OC Modeling in May of 2014. I wish I had been with them from the start. It would have saved me tons of issues.

OC Modeling was run by Sandra and Anthony. Sandra quickly became a mother figure in my life. Unlike other agents in the industry, I truly believed she cared about me. I didn't feel like just a bunch of dollar signs to her. She always had my best interest in mind and got me the best rates. All of girls in the agency even referred to her as "Mommas" because she was known to be such a good caretaker of us performers. I wasn't worried about her understanding why I couldn't make the party.

I woke up the next morning on my hotel room floor next to the bed. There were pieces of chicken tenders around my pillow and what looked like nacho cheese. I didn't remember eating, but that was the least of my worries.

I had so many missed calls from my agent, my friends, and Alex. Everyone was wondering where the hell I was. After letting everyone know I was fine, it was time to get ready to do it all over again. I decided to take it easy that day so I could make it to the party that night. It was the annual "white party," which was considered a big deal.

I was hungover that morning, but it was nothing I couldn't handle. I had slept for sixteen hours and the worst of it was gone. I was done signing at the booth by 5:00 p.m., so it was time to let loose. I finished the bottle of tequila and the rest of my ball of cocaine before the party started. In a state of panic, I texted everyone in my phone asking if they knew a dealer in Vegas. I offered my dealer in LA an extra five hundred if he would drive to me, but he wasn't down for a road trip.

A friend of mine met me in my room to sell me a gram. I knew it wouldn't last me very long, but it would do for now. Jenna and I met up to go to the white party together, and we had fun dancing naked on the couches.

It was a nightclub in the Hard Rock full of porn stars so there really weren't any rules. The only problem with this white party was that I had no more white. I needed to get my hands on coke.

I told everyone I would be right back, but I knew I wouldn't return. With my heels in hand, I ran through the casino barefoot in a short white dress without any panties on. It was about a five-minute walk from the nightclub to my room, and I was halfway there when I heard someone yelling my name. They were using my actual name, not my porn name, which meant it could only be one person.

Alex was chasing after me. I was so busy partying that I didn't pay my phone any mind. He had been calling me for hours, letting me know he was on his way and asking where to meet me. The poor guy was trying to find me in the giant hotel.

I jumped into his arms and he knew I was already trashed. The agreement was that I would wait until he was there to start partying, but I was too out of control to listen. We went back to my room together so I could get more coke delivered to me. Sure enough, I found more, and once we had it, I didn't feel like going back to the white party.

My friend Johnny, who lived in Vegas, had invited us to a party at his hotel, so I decided we would take him up on that offer—the reason being I knew there were going to be drugs in full supply. I gathered up a few porn girls and a male porn performer I was close with to join us, and sure enough, the first thing I spotted when I walked in was a pile of cocaine on the counter. I helped myself with no hesitation.

There were around ten people already at Johnny's suite, but the atmosphere was chill. Music was playing, but no one was dancing. I decided to change that. I pulled my equally drunk friend into the middle of the living room with me and started to eat her out and twerk all over her. We danced the night away, while Alex got acquainted with Johnny.

Alex was pissed that I had relapsed, but he'd known it was going to happen. Eventually, his attitude went from upset to "fuck it." By midnight, Alex was shitfaced with me and even started chain-smoking cigarettes with me on the balcony. I found it hilarious because he never smoked or drank to extreme, but at the same time I wanted to make sure he didn't drink too much, and the last thing I remember is telling all the guys to keep an eye on him because he didn't normally act like this.

January 24, 2015

I DON'T REMEMBER WHEN we left or how we left. However, I woke up Saturday afternoon in my hotel room next to Alex. That was a relief.

I had the worst hangover of my entire life, which was impressive. I was supposed to be signing at my booth, but I slept in. Stepping out of bed, the first thing I had to do was throw up. I was still so fucked up that I could barely walk. "Nauseated" was an understatement. It felt like I had thrown up over a gallon of stomach vile. My head was pounding so hard that I couldn't even make conversation with Alex.

After turning on the water, I lay on the shower floor crying. My depression from the coke withdrawal was uncontrollable. I wanted to die. I had never felt this terrible in my life. I switched back and forth from lying down to being on my hands and knees while I continued to puke down the shower drain.

I vividly remember lying in that shower, looking blankly at the wall, thinking how I was a waste of a life. I didn't want to live like this anymore. I didn't want to live at all. I was in the deepest depression I had ever felt. How was I supposed to attend the AVN Awards that night? I had Alex text my agent Sandra that I was too hungover to sign. I knew she would be upset, but I was in too much pain to care about the expo.

When I got out of the shower, I went back to sleep until Alex woke me up at 5:00 p.m. to get ready for the award show. I couldn't bail because I was supposed to present an award. I had already gone to the rehearsal, and I knew I couldn't flake on the biggest night of the year if I ever wanted to be a part of AVN again.

I had only an hour to get ready. For how absolutely horrible I felt, I put myself together nicely. When I look back at the red carpet photos from that night, I can't even tell I was hungover.

I remember I couldn't even be interviewed on the red carpet because I had no voice. It hurt to whisper. I didn't want to talk anyway. I was sick to my stomach and just wanted to concentrate on not throwing up in front of everyone. The only time I spoke that evening was when I had to present the award for "Best Anal Scene."

"Anal is the Lamborghini of sex" was my big line.

When I opened up the envelope alongside Jessica Drake, I jumped with excitement when I saw who won.

"Jenna Couture!" I screamed into the microphone. Jessica was supposed to announce the winner, but I couldn't contain myself.

I helped Jenna on stage and gave her a huge kiss. I was so proud of her.

Once I presented my award, I knew I was free to leave the ceremony. Alex was waiting in the room for me because he didn't have a red carpet pass.

I wanted to go home.

I never wanted to drink again.

I never wanted to use again.

And I never did...

◆◆◆

THE FIRST YEAR OF sobriety was hard. I was triggered often but remained strong. I was actually committed to staying sober this time. Sure, I had wanted to get sober for years, but I wasn't ready to commit to it.

I'm not sure what made this time different. I had a man who loved me and treated me well; for once I felt like I had a future to look forward to. I was ready to get my act together.

To hold myself accountable, I decide to announce on all of my social media platforms that I was getting clean and sober. This helped me a lot when I was triggered because if I relapsed, I would let the whole world know I failed. I had something to prove and I knew people didn't think I could do it. It motivated me to stay strong during moments of weakness.

I deleted all of my drug dealers and drug connections in my phonebook. I also deleted them out of my call log so I couldn't go back and try to find the numbers. I even had to delete my friends' numbers.

One of the hardest parts about getting sober was eliminating the users from my life. I could no longer hang out with my friends. I had zero sober friends, so the only person I hung out with was Alex—who, being the amazing man that he is, got sober with me. He didn't have an alcohol problem, but he knew that in order for me to stay sober, he would have to be sober as well. He didn't mind. He actually said he didn't want to drink anymore either.

It made sobriety easier having a partner who was making the changes with me. The only trigger I had left in my life was work. It wasn't rare to see a girl doing drugs on set, but that didn't trigger me as much as industry events, where I would carry around a Red Bull so that I wasn't empty-handed during the night. If I really felt triggered to drink, I would allow myself to smoke a cigarette. That was my vice. If even a smoke couldn't kill the temptation to drink, I would simply leave the event. I put my sobriety first.

I was finally feeling in a good place in my life. Not only was I doing great with sobriety, I was taking care of my body in other ways. The gym became my second home, and I constantly worked on my health and fitness. I started a clean diet and tracked all of my food that I ate. I enjoyed taking care of myself, something I had never done before.

As I got sober, I became more successful in porn. I no longer was too hungover to go to work and was no longer canceling scenes.

Position of Power

I WAS NOW MAKING considerably more than I had been with any of the other agencies. While California Models would book me boy/girl scenes for as low as $600, I was now getting $1,200. I also started doing anal and double-penetration scenes, which would earn me over $2,000 per scene.

I was presented with the biggest opportunity of my career that March. It was a huge deal for a performer and a huge accomplishment that I honestly never thought I would get to experience. When my agent presented me with the offer, I couldn't say yes quickly enough. She told me what the project would entail, and I found out I would get to shoot five different scenes. After having a meeting and going into the details, I was ecstatic to get started. I felt a sense of relief, feeling like I was finally "making it" in porn.

I was familiar with the company I was shooting the project for, but I had only shot one scene with them previously—a blowjob scene. The cameraman, Jordan, was also the director, and he shot all of their scenes. The first time I was on his set, I took a nap upstairs in the shooting house while I waited for the current scene to get done filming. I was extremely hungover that morning, and I woke up to his dick slapping me on the head.

He had already said sexual things to me via direct messages on Twitter, and I always flirted back—not because I was interested, but because I hoped he would book me for a scene if I responded.

This was my first experience with a director coming on to me and I didn't know how to react. I just did as he asked and sucked his dick. I kept nervously giggling, telling him I needed to save my throat for my scene. Not that Jordan's dick could have damaged my throat. It must be so unfortunate to be a black man and not live up to the penis stereotype.

I did not want to suck this man's dick. I hated sucking dick for free, but I did it anyway because I didn't want to get on his bad side. He was a director, which meant he was one of my employers. I did what I had to do to get my check at the end of the day with no problems.

It bothered me a little bit, but it wasn't anything I felt traumatized by—more like annoyed. I didn't think it was a big enough deal to bring it up to my agent, Sandra. I did end up telling Alex, though, as soon as he picked me up. He was furious and thought it was a way bigger deal than I did. I told him he could not say anything to Jordan or confront him because it could cost me jobs.

The way I thought of it was, it was already my job to suck a dick that day. How could I really complain about sucking another dick? That was literally what I did for a living.

When I told Alex about the career opportunity I was presented with, he was thrilled. When I told him that Jordan was going to be involved, he was less than thrilled. He was worried about me getting taken advantage of, but I told him it didn't matter. I could handle it. I was willing to go through some sexual harassment for this exposure if I had to. It was a big opportunity.

I got to choose what talent I wanted to work with for every scene, which I was most excited about. There were so many girls and guys that I was dying to get my hands on. I got most of the talent I requested for each scene. Things were going smoothly, but then it was time to actually shoot.

I encountered sexual harassment all five days I was on set. At the beginning, it was more annoying than anything. By the end, I couldn't wait until it was wrapped so that I never had to talk to Jordan again.

Day one of shooting was a three-way scene. I was pretty much drooling over the fact I got to hook up with my favorite female porn star that day. I had fantasized about working with this superstar for years and I couldn't believe it was finally coming true. After we got our makeup done, it was time to head to location.

Jordan told his production assistant to drive the other talent over to the set and that we would meet them there. I instantly felt uncomfortable. He locked the door behind them and pushed me onto his desk.

Never one to lose my cool on set, I started laughing, saying things like, "stop, let's go." It didn't faze him. He already had his dick out, and he started jacking off while trying to take my pants off.

"Seriously, let's go. Stop it." I repeated different phrases of that nature for five minutes while he kept trying to pry his way into my panties.

Finally, I found something to make him stop. "I'm on my period and I don't have a sponge in yet," I said. He put his dick back in his pants and we headed over to set. He told me to tell him when I had a sponge in so we could "finish what we started."

After pictures were done, we had a break to get ready for the sex scene.

Sure enough, Jordan cornered me in a private room, asking for a quickie. After thirty seconds of fingering me as I politely kept telling him, "stop, no, we have to shoot," I wiggled away from him.

The second scene was an anal scene. Jordan and I were the only ones in the studio while he did my pretty girl pictures. We were waiting for the male talent to arrive on set when he had sex with me against the white wall that I had just been photographed in front of. I kept telling him I didn't want to get sore because I had to shoot my scene, but he didn't care—he fucked my ass without permission.

I handled my discomfort with laughter every time. I felt like I couldn't stand up for myself and slap him across the face like I was dying to do on the inside. He was producing this project. If I wanted to have this opportunity, I had to please the director. There were many times when I told him "no." I said it multiple times, but it was always in a playful way rather than a demanding way.

It was very clear I was uncomfortable, but he knew he was in a position of power. I lucked out on the third day, a girl/girl scene with Jenna. She was the victim of his sexual harassment. I walked in on him eating her out while she was telling him to knock it off and laughing.

I wasn't sure how she felt about his advances, but we talked about it when our scene was over. She asked me for a ride because she was too scared to have Jordan drive her back to her car. She told me she knew he was going to try to have sex with her if she went with him.

I realized it wasn't just me that Jordan was interested in—it was anyone and everyone. I started to talk to other porn girls when I saw them on other sets and asked them about Jordan. It seemed like everyone had a story about him trying to force himself on them.

I felt disgusted, but I still had two scenes left to film before my movie was over. I had already been through the worst of it. He had me suck his dick in front of the male talent for the fourth day on set. I think he wanted to brag to the male talent that I was sucking his dick too. It surprised me that he was doing this sexual activity with me so openly.

Did I forget to mention that Jordan was married? Not just married to anyone—married to one of the hottest porn stars of all time. I so badly wanted to let her know what was going on, but who knew if she would even believe me? I didn't want to look like a fool, and it wasn't worth risking my career over. I kept quiet about Jordan's actions publicly.

When we were done filming and the project was going to be released soon, I finally confided in Sandra. I told her how I never wanted to work for him again because he was forcing himself on me. She told me that other girls had recently started to complain about the same thing, so she would take it up with the owner of the company. She told him he needed to watch his director because they were bound to face sexual harassment charges if he didn't stop.

I never shot for Jordan again.

The project that I worked on this for was the number one seller on Adult DVD Talk for two weeks in a row, and it was nominated at the AVN Awards.

Even though things behind the scenes weren't so great, I was really proud of the job I did. Despite Jordan's harassment, things were going really well for me—and they were about to get even better.

Hoe & Housewife

ON MAY 17, 2015, Alex proposed to me. He popped the big question at the gym, which is very fitting for our relationship. I had a feeling something was going on when he insisted that we film our car ride to the gym. He was asking me lovey-dovey questions like, "How did you know you love me?" and, "Do you want to spend forever with me?" Alex has always been the more affectionate one in the relationship, so I'd brushed off the video as him being a hopeless romantic. I had no idea I was about to be proposed to.

I walked into LA Fitness as usual and punched in my phone number to check in. The employee at the counter told me something was wrong with my name in the system. I started to get visibly annoyed repeating how to spell my last name. "It must be under another last name." Before I had time to answer, Alex interrupted me. "I think I could help you with that," he said, and I turned around to see him down on one knee with a shiny diamond pointing in my direction. I couldn't say yes fast enough.

Alex did all of the right pre-proposal moves. He made sure my nails were done perfectly, he made sure someone was going to take photos of the moment he proposed, and most importantly, he got my dad's permission. My dad had always hated every man I had ever dated. It brought such a wave of happiness over me that my dad was confident enough to give permission for us to wed. I was one happy fiancée.

There was one issue, however, that we had yet to tackle: his parents. All his parents knew about me was that I was a porn star. All his parents had seen of me was my provocative Instagram feed. I didn't blame them for not wanting me in Alex's life. Up until our engagement, they wanted nothing to do with me. It wasn't until Alex broke the news that I'd be in his life forever that they realized they might as well get it over with and meet me.

Meeting his parents was one of the most nerve-racking experiences of my life. Alex's family is the polar opposite of mine. I come from a small town, a simple life, where we shopped at Walmart and grew up not having any money. Alex grew up in beautiful large homes in Los Angeles, California, attending private schools and universities alongside the children of celebrities. I knew I would be the black sheep entering their family. Here I was, tattooed, uneducated, and out of place, stepping into a family of brains, money, and class. I knew at first glance, I didn't live up to what they'd hoped they would get in a daughter-in-law. All I did was pray they would give me a chance long enough to know the real me and see that I loved and cared about their son. To see I wasn't an evil person or some degenerate just because I did porn.

To my surprise, I was welcomed with opened arms into the van de Bunt family. Once they learned of our engagement, I was invited to all holiday dinners and family vacations. I still felt like I stuck out like a sore thumb, but I was thrilled that I would be accepted into their family.

Our engagement lasted less than a month before we decided to just drive to Vegas and elope. Alex was joining the Navy, and if we weren't married by the time he went to boot camp, I wouldn't be able to move with him. It did feel rushed, but I didn't have a doubt in my mind that it wasn't the right decision. I loved Alex and knew I wanted my future to be with him.

Never in my life did I think I would have a "Vegas Wedding," but things don't always go as planned—in case you haven't been following along. I always dreamed of a big fancy wedding with me in a long white dress. I longed for my dad to walk me down the aisle, to have my husband watch me walk toward the altar, but I never got that.

Even though it was just the two of us saying our vows in a little room, we both cried. I wasn't expecting the tears at all. At the time, I thought that we would eventually have a "real" wedding, so I wasn't too emotionally invested in the Vegas wedding. We thought we would have a wedding with family and guests the following summer, on our one-year anniversary, but now that Alex was in the Navy, decisions weren't his to be made anymore.

I used to be bitter that I would never get my fairytale wedding, but now I'm relieved. Not only did we save tons of money and stress, the marriage reflected our relationship. Simple and spontaneous.

Repeating back the vows on June 3, 2015, I broke down crying. I was marrying the love of my life. It didn't matter who was watching or what I was wearing—what mattered was that I had found my perfect person. I had a man who loved me for exactly who I was. Afterward, most couples have a fancy ceremony following the wedding, but Alex and I shared a milkshake and nachos before heading back to LA. It was fun and laid-back. I loved it.

Alex has never tried to change me. When we got married, I continued as an active porn performer and escort—he didn't mind. Not once has he ever asked me to quit or to stop being who I am. He supports my career and is my biggest fan. I couldn't ask for a more supportive spouse. It takes a strong man to be able to date, let alone marry, someone in the adult industry.

Following our marriage, Alex decided to announce it on his social media. Alex simply posted a meme. It was a photo of a magician performing onstage. The caption read, "For my next trick, I shall turn this hoe into a housewife." It was a huge hit.

Cutting Ties

I T WAS TIME FOR Alex to experience the train wreck known as my mother. He was the one who had encouraged me to rekindle any sort of relationship with the woman, so I was willing to let him experience her firsthand.

My two sisters, Alex, and I decided to go to Pensacola, Florida, to visit my mom for a week. We warned Alex about her, but he wasn't worried.

A "vacation" to see my mom always went the same way. The first two days were great. She would be normal and happy. By day three, the real her would start to emerge. You could always guarantee that before the week was over, there would be at least one major breakdown.

Sure enough, by day five, Alex got to see the version of my mother we had all warned him about. As my mom texted and drove with us in the car, she swerved into the next lane and we were so close to getting hit. As my mom slammed on the brakes, we could feel the wind—from the other vehicle being so close—shake our entire car.

My sister, who was sitting in the back seat, right where we almost got hit, instantly burst into tears. She sobbed loudly as she had almost just gotten seriously injured in a car accident because of my mother's texting.

Instead of asking if she was okay and pulling over like most caring parents, my mom continued to drive another ten minutes while rolling her eyes and bitching that it wasn't her fault. Completely ignoring the fact her child was traumatized, bawling in the back seat.

I couldn't handle it anymore. I asked my mom to stop at Starbucks so my sister could calm down and get out of the vehicle.

"Your daughter is crying and you don't even care to check on her?" I asked once the car was in park.

My mom got out of the car and screamed at us all, "YOU GUYS TREAT ME LIKE SHIT!" For so many years we'd wanted to tell her how shitty she treated all of us, and now she was lobbing accusations at us—and all because we acknowledged the fact that she was ignoring my sister who was terrified and crying.

We locked ourselves in the Starbucks bathroom to call my dad for advice on what to do.

He was used to these phone calls every trip, and he offered to pay for a hotel so we could get out of there to somewhere safe. We refused to get back in the car with her, and my mom's boyfriend had to meet us so we could drive his car back to our mom's house.

When we got back to her house, my mom was somewhere between screaming and crying about how she was going to hang herself from the tree in the backyard. Not even five minutes later, she was knocking on the door asking if we had any dirty laundry as if nothing had just happened. She was a certified nutjob.

When my mom dropped off Alex and me at the airport, I had no idea that was going to be the last time I ever saw her.

The first thing Alex said to me when we left was, "There is no way I will ever let that woman around our children."

I agreed. As much as I wanted a mother-daughter relationship, it was never going to happen. It was time I let go of the fantasy of her ever being the mom I needed.

I had been hurting my entire life, wondering why she didn't care for me like other moms cared for their children. All of my self-destructive behavior stemmed from the pain not having a mother caused me. To this day, I am heartbroken by the fact I didn't have a mother growing up.

I daydream about what it would have been like to have her around. I daydream about what it would have been like if I'd gotten a different mom, a "normal" mom. I don't think I'll ever truly heal from the pain it has caused me.

I was married now, and I knew that in the near future I wanted children. I vowed I wouldn't let her near my babies. I refused to expose my children to her toxic behavior. And so it was only a matter of time before I cut her off for good—I just had to figure out the right timing.

I would get the perfect opportunity that following Christmas. My mom's boyfriend proposed to her and she texted me asking if I would be her maid of honor. I don't know why that got under my skin so much, but it did.

I was stunned. This was a woman who abused me for the first half of my childhood, then abandoned me the second half. Every interaction I'd had with her since then had been a negative experience.

We never even spoke, other than the random text every month or two. She wanted me to be her maid of honor? To throw parties in her honor? To help her out and be there for her? How dare she want me to be there for her when she was never there for me?

It bothered me more every time I thought about it, which was constantly. How dare she? What kind of delusional world did she live in where she thought I would be her maid of honor? I was tired of my mom using me only when she got something out of it. She didn't want anything to do with me unless she could find a way to benefit off of me.

I decided that the next day was the day I would finally confront my mother with the truth of her actions. I kept writing and deleting trying to word everything I wanted to say perfectly. I was nervous to let go of the fantasy of ever having a mother, but I knew it was time.

"This is going to be hard to send...I don't know if you have convinced yourself you have done no wrong in our lives but the abuse you caused me will never be something I can get rid of. My earliest memories are being terrified of you, of you yelling at me and threatening me. I have tried to forgive you for decades but it's hard to forgive someone who never has took blame or acknowledged their wrong doing. You were a terrible mother and we had no female figure to run to while growing up. You had nothing to do with our lives and now want to act like everything is okay. You ask us to be your bridesmaids and expect us to be all happy for you & be there? Where were you our whole lives? I have been asking for my belongings back from you for 3 years and you couldn't even send them when I had postage PAID already for you, but you expect me to be your maid of honor and be there for you. You ruined a lot of my life with the damage you caused me but I refuse to let it go on any longer. I refuse to let my children one day be effected by you like I was. I have waited years and YEARS for you to be a mother figure. I've waited years for you to apologize for being the awful person you were to me when I was young. But you never will do that and that's something I've came to accept. It kills me every day and I want a mother so bad. When I met Alex he told me to rekindle things with you, so I did, but once he seen the type of person you truly were, he was very shocked and took back his statement. I don't want my kids to be yelled at, neglected, threatened, or terrified ever... And that's why I could not trust them with you. I can not keep up this charade any longer that nothing is wrong. You have had so many chances to confront the past, but you choose not to. You don't think you could of done that for any of us? We grew up thinking our mom would kill us and having to go through years of therapy because of you. I cried when dad would leave because I was so scared to be alone with you. You would yell and say terrible things to me, THOSE are my first memories of life. Can you blame me for resenting you? You were supposed to be my mother, the person I could trust and run to. Not the person I ran from. You will probably be defensive and act like you were a great mother but maybe one day you can step down from being so selfish to realize you missed out on having 3 wonderful daughters in your life. Not one of us think of you as a mother, and that is something you will have to live with. I would love to have a good relationship and I have tried so many times, but at this point it is exhausting to continue. I have been bottling this up my entire life & it's time someone said it."

She replied admitting that she knew she wasn't a wonderful mother, blaming her own childhood as to why she wasn't there for us. I didn't bother to reply. I knew there was nothing we could talk about that could change the past.

The next morning, I woke up to an email from her that revealed her true side. She started off nice, expressing that she knew my feelings were my feelings but that she also had to tell me how she felt. She took fault saying she made many mistakes in my childhood and that she was aware she had anger management issues. The next thing she had to say was such a stab to the heart: she brought up my abortion and my career. Bringing up my abortion was a slap in the face. She knew that was a sensitive topic and it made me despise her even more. She then went on to tell me how hard I am on her.

By this point in the message, I was already heated. Hard on her? I gave her twenty-some years to change and be there for me, desperately wanting a mother in my life. She didn't support my sister and me financially or emotionally my entire life. She never had any responsibilities to the three humans she created, but apparently, *I* was being too hard on *her* for wanting to confront my childhood abuse. I couldn't believe what I was reading. It got even worse.

In the next paragraph, she blamed my sisters and me for her drinking again after she had been sober for a few weeks. She was twisting things to try to make me feel guilty, but as a recovering addict myself, I knew that she was putting blame on us to make her feel justified for her own relapse. I was internally screaming at this point. Apparently having her daughters in her life for an entire five days had thrown her into a "nervous breakdown" and caused her to start drinking again. This is coming from the same person that bought me, her recovering daughter, a bottle of Patron for Christmas.

She ended her message by telling me that other people have had it way worse than me.

I was furious. I didn't even know which part to be angriest about. She made herself the victim, as she always found a way to do. What mom purposely moves away from her three children? Especially when one is only a newborn? My dad told us she'd said she was moving away to start "her own family." That's how little we meant to her. We would visit every other year or so and we would have a horrible couple of days dealing with our mom's violent outbursts.

In fact, let's start calling her Kim, because I do not even want to acknowledge her as my mother when she had nothing to do with raising me. Kim was the most manipulative woman on the planet. She could twist anything into being everyone else's fault but her own. She could never own up to her actions and admit she was wrong.

I had wanted to confront Kim for years about everything she did to me (and didn't do for me), for as long as I could remember, but I was terrified of this exact thing happening. My worst nightmare was that she would manipulate the situation so that I was the bad guy, and that's exactly what happened.

Her whole reply made me furious. I had been hoping she would finally give me the closure I needed to forgive her for the past, but now there was no way I could.

I told her not to contact me further, and she told me that I was a petty, resentful, little girl and added that if I was happy in my marriage, I wouldn't be worried about my relationship with her. That's Kim for you, though. Just minutes after claiming to be a wonderful mother and a changed woman, she's calling her daughter names for having expressed her pain.

I blocked her on email, text message, and all social media. I haven't spoken to her since and I absolutely never will.

If I ever have a moment of weakness in which I start to think maybe things could be different...I read her emails and

KARMEN   AMBER VAN DE BUNT

know she will never change. It still hurts, but I've accepted the fact that she is not a mother.

I terminated that toxic relationship once and for all, and it felt like a weight off my shoulders. I knew I had made the right decision and it was absolutely therapeutic to state all of my bottled-up emotions to her. I'd held in those words for twenty-three long years.

My poisonous relationship with Kim was terminated. My poisonous relationship with drugs and alcohol was terminated.

I was a married woman and successful in my career. Of course, if that success were in any other field besides the adult industry, I would be given praise and looked up to by society, but because it was porn, I was looked down upon and criticized— even by my own family. But what mattered most was that I was proud of myself and proud of the progress I had made.

Leaving Porn

As much as I loved the adult industry, I felt like I had hit a point in my life where it no longer served me. I wasn't enjoying the work as much as I used to. In fact, I started to dread it. Now that I was performing such hardcore scenes, it was taking a toll on my body. Preparing for an anal scene is a grueling process. I would eat dinner the night before and that was my last meal until my scene the next day was done. Sometimes we wouldn't get finished until 8:00 p.m., and I would go over a day without eating while having to perform my best on camera.

Not only would I be hungry, but I would be severely dehydrated and drained from the cleaning process. The night before my scene, I would use a shower enema to *completely* empty myself out. This took around two hours.

The morning of the shoot, I would take Imodium and only drink water. The Imodium would back me up, and then it was time to repeat the process the next day to prepare for another anal scene. I started to find myself very dizzy and seeing stars on set. Even posing for photos would make me feel like I was going to pass out.

For one of the last scenes in my porn career, we had to take a cut because I passed out from the male talent choking me. Usually I could handle the choking with the best of them, but my body was not agreeing with me anymore.

I was in the process of trying to get my agent to find me a deal for my first gangbang scene when Alex left for Navy boot camp. He was always proud of my hustle and my drive. He never told me I wasn't allowed to do anything. We have a very secure and trusting relationship.

Alex was gone for eight weeks, and this left me with a lot of time to think. I knew that when he was done, we would have to move. He would be stationed somewhere for his Navy schooling.

That left me with two choices: I could commute back and forth to LA for work to continue my career. The second choice was to retire from pornography and start a new life.

Before Alex left, we talked about how badly we wanted a child together. Of course, there was no way this would be possible as long as I worked in the porn industry. But because it was my body and my career, Alex left the decision up to me.

I started to see my therapist more regularly. I was so conflicted on what to do with my life. I needed someone to guide me to make the right decision.

Nothing traumatic happened that made me want to leave the industry. I love the porn industry and the people in it. The directors, my agent, and the performers are all like family to me.

Sure, I wasn't enjoying it as much as I used to, but no one loves their job 100 percent of the time.

I had many reasons I didn't want to quit. For starters, I was becoming very popular. I was gracing the cover of almost every Jules Jordan movie that was coming out, and I was in the process of possibly getting my second showcase for a gangbang movie. Most girls retired when they were no longer getting work, but I was getting more bookings than ever before. I also was making so much money on the side by escorting on my off days.

When you can make $10,000 in a week, it is very hard to quit. But ever since I got clean and sober, I had been saving money like crazy. I had saved $50,000 in less than a year. And this was during my luxury spending and high bills. I was living beyond comfortably and wasn't sure if I was willing to give that up.

On the other hand, my gut kept telling me that it was time to retire. I had as many reasons for wanting to quit as I did for wanting to stay. I took us having to move as a sign that I could start a brand-new chapter. If I retired and we moved to a new place, it allowed for a new start.

Alex had been so patient and understanding our entire relationship. I was ready to settle down so we could start a family. Could I really be a housewife and a mother? My whole life I had been the crazy party girl, or the stripper, or the porn star. I wasn't sure if I could ever live a "normal" life. But I pictured our new life and I envisioned us with a baby.

I felt ready.

For weeks, I went back and forth with different scenarios to my therapist. She never pushed me one way or another. She offered her opinions and tried to get me to see all of my options.

She asked me if I had to only choose one—to keep shooting porn or to have a family—which one would I choose. I closed my eyes and thought about my happiness with each choice.

Money, fame, and attention were part of the life I had been living for so long. I loved everything about it—but was that where true happiness lay? Eventually looks fade or people will get sick of you. New girls are always pouring into the industry, and who was to say that I would still be relevant in a year or two?

Porn isn't a long-term career. I think of it now as a short-term job to make long-term revenue. If you play your career right and build a large following, you can continue to make money off your fan base for as long as you work at it. With the Internet, there are so many ways to make extra cash. Amateur websites, selling your worn clothing, finding money slaves, XXX Snapchat subscriptions, shooting content for your own website and/or company.

The list goes on and on.

But this was the perfect opportunity to start a family. Porn would always be there if I desired to go back one day, but I couldn't have a baby with my husband until I gave up porn.

It started to become very clear that my heart lay with the choice of retiring.

My therapist was very proud of me for my decision and we came up with a plan to make my exit. I was still booked for the next ten days, so I would finish those scenes and then retire.

It was very nerve-racking when I decided to tell my agent. I was scared she was going to get mad at me. I was afraid of how she would handle it. To my surprise, Sandra was excited and kept congratulating me.

She approved of Alex and was happy to hear we wanted to start a family together. She told me that it was better to leave the industry while I was up than when I was down. It was bittersweet to me, because I still knew I had at least a couple good years left in me.

I couldn't wait to tell Alex about my decision. While he was in boot camp, he had no Internet or phone access. The only means of communication was by handwritten letters. Each day I would send him a long letter telling him how much he was missed and how my day went.

I couldn't wait for him to read that day's letter. He told me when he read the sentence that I was retiring, he instantly started crying. He was happy for me and for us.

I prepared a blog for my website and my Twitter on March 31, the day of my last scene. I planned on not telling anyone that it was my last day, but once I got on set, I couldn't help but share the news with the director and my female talent.

The director that day was Jackie St. James, and she had always been one of my favorite directors to work for. She was happy for me but said she would miss me. That was the same way I felt.

I enjoyed every minute of my last day on set. I knew I was going to miss rolling my big porn suitcase in and out of luxury houses. I would miss gossiping with the makeup artists as they got me pretty for the day. I would miss posing in front of the camera. I would miss acting out my scenes and having passionate, wild sex. I would miss seeing my face on box covers and magazines. I would miss standing on the red carpet for a swarm of photographers.

It was a painful decision to make, but it was the right one. I couldn't grow if I didn't move on. It was time to start the next chapter of my life.

When I got home from my last day filming porn, I immediately did two things.

Firstly, I went into my saved drafts and published my blog announcing my retirement.

Secondly, I threw away my damn birth control.

Vienna Waits for You

Two months after I retired, we were living in Pensacola, Florida. It's funny how things come full circle sometimes. The place I worked so hard to leave was exactly where the Navy had chosen to station Alex.

It was the night of May 31 when I felt extremely nauseated. I had only felt this type of thing once before. When I threw up, I instantly knew I was pregnant.

When Alex got home from work, I told him my suspicions. He thought there was no way it was possible since I hadn't been getting my period, which we had blamed on the fact that I had prepped and competed in a fitness competition for the NPC. For seventeen weeks prior to show day, I worked out three hours a day and ate a strict diet. I ate chicken, broccoli, oats, and sweet potatoes every single day for 120 straight days.

I hadn't gotten my period in over two months, and we figured it was because of my drastic weight loss. Since I did not get my period in April, that month could very well have been due to my grueling diet and exercise program, but the reason I didn't get my period in May was because I was indeed pregnant.

I waited until Alex went to work the next morning to take a pregnancy test. It was six in the morning and he had duty for a few hours. I kept waking up all night because I needed to find out if I was pregnant or not.

Only moments after peeing on the pregnancy test, the word "PREGNANT" appeared loud and clear. My hand went over my mouth and I remember squealing "Oh my God!" as I instantly burst into tears of joy.

I ran into the living room jumping up and down and staring at that word. Pregnant. I wanted to share the news with Alex, but he wouldn't be home for a couple of hours.

Instead of blowing up his phone with messages freaking out and spilling the beans, I decided I would wait until he got home. Those were the longest hours of my life.

"YOU + ME = THREE."

I placed the note on the front door. I wanted to give him a hint before he got inside the apartment.

When he walked through that door, I couldn't wait even a second more. "I'M PREGNANT!" I screamed as I jumped into his arms. He had the best reaction I could have ever hoped for. I had my camera set up to capture the whole thing. We kissed and stared at the test together in disbelief.

We were planning on having our "trying period" start after my fitness competition, but we didn't even make it to the trying period. We later found out we'd conceived our baby on

Karmen

May 3, which was the first day I met Alex down in Pensacola. The Navy flew him straight down from boot camp while I had to drive my car and our belongings from California to meet him out there.

I thought it was beautiful that our first time reunited in Florida, I got pregnant instantly. It made me feel so confident in my decision to quit porn, like this was all truly meant to be.

I felt even more so like it was meant to be when the doctor told us my due date: January 24—which was also the anniversary of our sobriety.

This also meant that I was five weeks pregnant on stage at my fitness competition. On the one hand, I won in both of the categories I competed in while pregnant. I thought it was funny I could tell my child one day that they were in my belly in a fitness show.

On the other hand, I started to get worried. In preparation for my competition, I was taking four fat burners and up to nine diuretics a day. Instant panic and guilt came over me that I may have harmed my baby in some way.

Of course, if I had known I was pregnant, I would never have taken them. Fortunately, my baby was perfectly healthy and had no issues due to my supplement use.

As the weeks went on, I was getting closer to finding out my baby's gender. Alex had no preference over whether we had a boy or a girl, and I told myself I didn't mind either—but the truth was that I was dying for a little girl.

All of my life I had looked forward to having a daughter. I always felt like that was the one thing I knew I had purpose for. Ever since I was little, I wanted to be a mom so I could give my daughter what she deserved. I wanted to be everything that Kim was not. I would give my daughter the mother-daughter relationship that every girl deserved. I would make her feel loved and cared for. She would never have to wonder why her mommy didn't love her.

So much of my life had been spent self-destructing due to the fact I never had a mother in my life. It was something that bothered me as long as I could remember. I knew if I was good for anything in my lifetime, it was being a mom.

At sixteen weeks pregnant, I went to a gender reveal ultrasound tech to find out what I was having.

"It's a girl!"

I repeatedly asked her, "Are you sure?" before I screamed out in celebration.

I finally was going to have my little Vienna.

I was fourteen years old when I picked out the name Vienna for my future daughter. This was ten years prior to my actually getting pregnant. Crazy enough, I did end up using the name "Vienna" after all of those years.

I'd chosen the name while watching the movie *13 Going On 30*. There was a scene that played Billy Joel's "Vienna Waits For You," and it was the first time I had ever heard it. At that time, I had no idea Vienna was a city—I just instantly fell in love with the word. I loved the way it sounded. It was so elegant and beautiful. I decided right then that one day I would name my baby Vienna.

When I first met Alex, I mentioned early on that one day I wanted a daughter named Vienna. He loved the name, thank God. In dark times, Alex would attempt to cheer me up with things like, "Just think about baby Vienna one day" or "Everything will get better. One day you will have Vienna in your arms, and everything will be all right."

Our Ebay username was even "viennavdb."

When we found out we were having a girl, there was no question what her name would be. We didn't even need to have that discussion. We both knew it was our little Vienna.

For a middle name we chose Anne, in honor of Alex's deceased aunt. She had passed away after a long battle with cancer, and I absolutely loved the idea of naming Vienna after such a wonderful woman.

My pregnancy was not an easy one and I counted down the days until my baby was in my arms. On her due date, Vienna was showing no signs of wanting to come out. The doctor scheduled an induction for a week after my due date.

Just hours before my scheduled induction, I went into labor. I couldn't believe it was finally happening. I was about to meet my daughter.

After twenty-four hours of labor, Vienna was born. I vividly remember the first moments I saw her. They immediately placed her on top of me to do skin-to-skin. I wanted her right away and I didn't care about them cleaning her off beforehand.

Vienna was a little warm ball of mush, lying on top of me and screaming. She was so tiny and fragile, I had no idea how to hold her. She instantly gripped onto my finger with her small hand. My heart had never felt so full. I looked up at Alex and all I could say was, "Oh my God" as we exchanged teary-eyed looks.

I was a mother. And I was going to be the best mother. I couldn't stop staring at this tiny little human that I had created. I thought I had felt love before, but that paled in comparison to my love for Vienna.

Trying to sleep that night was impossible. Vienna was sound asleep in the clear hospital basinet next to my bed, but I couldn't stop studying her little face. I was in pure awe that my body had made her. She was everything I had ever wanted.

My mind flashed back to all of the times I wanted to die and all of the times that I had almost actually died. I wished I could go back in time and tell myself that one day, I would be a mother to a beautiful child and that I would find genuine happiness.

My husband was asleep on the hospital couch, my baby asleep by my side, and I couldn't believe this was my life. All of my hardships had brought me to this place. Maybe I needed to struggle to know how to survive. Maybe I needed to be hurt in order to know how not to hurt.

I knew I was going to give this little baby the best life I could, but most importantly, the best mother she could ever have. She was my antidepressant. How could I ever be sad when I look into her beautiful, healthy face?

My life had done a complete 180. I had the strength to defeat all of the obstacles that life had thrown my way.

I had health, love, and happiness.

I had overcome.

Epilogue

I KNEW THAT WHEN I decided to quit the adult industry, it wouldn't erase my past—I would always be known as "the porn star." The label will be with me as long as I live, and the Internet will never forget, and that is something I'd known I was signing up for when I first made the decision to do porn. I knew that there would not be many "normal" career opportunities as a tattooed ex-porn star, and that has always been okay with me. I have never and will never be a "normal" human being anyway. I have always chosen to live free and to do what I desire, regardless of how society might react. At the end of the day, people will always talk no matter what, so do what makes you happy.

As for me, I have never regretted doing porn, and I definitely don't regret quitting porn because it brought me my beautiful daughter. I chose to quit porn because I wanted to start a family—something I achieved.

I've always been an independent woman and I have always loved to make my own money. I enjoy the attention, money, and freedom of being a sex worker, and to that end, I eventually made the decision to return to the industry that I had once decided to step away from. I waited until Vienna was done breastfeeding, at eighteen months old, before making the decision.

In May 2018, I got the opportunity to return on my own terms. Brazzers, one of the biggest adult companies—if not *the* biggest—offered me an exclusive contract to do two shoots per month. The lighter schedule was perfect for me, as it's hard for me to be away from Vienna for even a few hours.

When I originally left the industry, I was feeling over-worked, physically and mentally drained. I accepted any shoot that my agent told me to. I worked for any company that wanted me, and I would perform sexual acts I didn't enjoy just to get a paycheck. I let people take advantage of me because I thought I needed them instead of realizing it was the other way around. I didn't want to experience that again. After talking to Alex, I decided that I would make sure I called the shots upon my reentry, and that I was not going to have an agent who told me what I should do.

I wanted to be my own boss, and so I opened my own company, KK Entertainment, and started producing my own content. I now make the majority of my income from my home office and don't have to shoot for other companies if I don't want to. I'm proud to be a successful entrepreneur—though it still falls second to the pride I take in being a mother.

I'm constantly asked what I'm going to tell my daughter one day. I can only hope that my daughter will love me for who I am—not judge me based on a job. I believe my sole purpose in life is to be a great mother, perhaps because I never had one. I care for her, provide for her, and give her my all every single day. I can only hope she will love me regardless.

I want to have a close and open relationship with my daughter. I hope to raise her to be a strong, independent woman as well. To have thick skin and to make *herself* happy. Of course, my first choice wouldn't be for her to follow in my footsteps, but I hope with the money I have already set aside for her college tuition, that she won't need to go the same route that I did, that she'll be able to choose her own path.

I want her life to be better than mine. In all aspects. I know that I'm an amazing mother, and at the end of the day, as long as Vienna agrees, that's the only thing that will matter.

I am thankful for my struggles because they made me strong. I accept not having a mother in my life because that circumstance inspired me to be the best mother I can possibly be. I believe that everything I faced was to make me a warrior. I can now take responsibility for my own life instead of feeling like a victim. My battle and my personal growth have made me a powerful woman and it was all a blessing in disguise. I no longer feel like I've been dealt a bad hand of cards. I know my struggles were handed to me because I was strong enough to conquer them— and I'm a better person now because of it.

Marrying A Porn Star

The following is written by my husband, Alex van de Bunt:

B UT, HOW ARE YOU okay with that?"

"You can't be married to someone in that industry."

"You must be some sort of freak."

You name it, and I've heard it. It comes with the territory when you date, and subsequently marry, a woman with my wife's profession.

Full disclosure: when I first heard that she and her friends were coming out that night to party with us at our table, the furthest thought from my mind was, "Tonight is the night I meet the woman I'm going to marry!"

As with most guys, the thought of partying with porn stars was pretty much at the top of the list; it was no different for me. That is, until the door to the elevator opened and my entire life changed.

She introduced herself to me as Karmen, but that night was the only time I ever knew her as that. She has always been my Amber, my small-town girl who was destined for more than her little town could offer her. She often remarked that it was weird hearing her "real" name come out of my mouth. I thought it was crazy that someone could go for so long and not hear their actual name.

After that first whirlwind of a night, I knew that she was different. All physical and sexual attributes aside, I had to have more. For anyone who has met her, Amber's presence and personality are intoxicating. With a single flash of her trademark smile and her loud devil-may-care laugh, you are drawn in and have no choice but to love her. However, underneath that incredible smile lies real pain. A pain that she covered up with her drug of choice...cocaine.

I had experience with coke; I worked in nightlife at the time and had seen deals being done and people with baggies. But I had never seen it being used in front of my eyes. My world was about to change.

During the first month or so, I didn't really realize how deep into her addiction she was. It seemed like only a bump or two getting ready for the club and maybe another one once we got there. She was living life, and I didn't see a drawback to her having a good time when we went out. I was living in a fantasy world. She had been using for a number of years at this point and had created a way to hide it from those she wanted to hide it from. It wasn't until we started spending more and more time together that I learned about her and her past and finally realized how bad her addiction was.

First it was a bump before shopping, and then two more while we were at the mall, followed by drinks at the bar in the mall. Then it was more before the club that night, then more during and after. It was to the point that I believe her habit was close to $1,000 a week.

The most devastating part of her cocaine use was the fact that it clashed with her Prozac, which she was taking at the highest dose possible. It turns out that the coke had effectively rendered the Prozac ineffective.

She would be up and down, angry and sad—and all of these emotions would be directed at me. It got so bad that once she hit me with a baseball bat in the apartment. She would fly off the handle at the tiniest problems and drive off or run down the street threatening to kill herself, and I would have to call the cops.

It was a devastating experience for me, having never truly dealt with a person suffering so severely from not just depression but a crippling addiction as well. Many nights I would think to myself: "Is this even worth it? Why are you with her? Why do you stay?"

The answer was always: "She's special—love her through this. She's worth it."

The party stories I have from our "crazy days," as I call them, are out of this world. The stuff out of movies. Naked cartwheels on helipads on top of buildings at 6:00 a.m., sex on top of cars in the middle of the street, naked after-parties. The moments when she was up were fun. But then would come the crippling depression and doubt and sadness. Until she got her fix again. It is truly the most upsetting experience that I've ever had, watching the person I love the most in the world go through something so tragically painful.

And then rock bottom.

I'll never forget it. I had called a therapist of mine crying, asking her what to do and how to help Amber with her addiction. She said she would call me back the next day and we could talk longer. Amber had mentioned wanting to get sober and we had talked about it, but I wanted it to be her decision.

The next day she had work, so we piled in the car and I drove her to set, as I always did. She hated driving in LA. When I dropped her off, the director came out and dapped me up, shot the shit, and then took her inside the house. I drove to my parents' house, which was maybe a mile up the road—gotta love the Valley! I waited there for a couple hours or so before heading back down to pick up Amber. I was early, so I was waiting in the car when I got a text or a phone call—I can't remember which. But it was her, saying that she can't do this anymore, and she needs to get sober no matter what.

Upon picking her up from the shoot, she was visibly shaken. After I asked what happened, she told me that the director had taken advantage of her. Due to her coming down from the night before, she was unable to fully defend herself. My heart dropped. I felt sick, angry, more upset than I had ever felt in my life.

Amber is the only woman in the world that could have taken this incredible negative and turned it into the catalyst for the most positive change in not only her life but in my life as well. Our journey, as you have no doubt read about in great detail from her chapters on it, was far from easy, with more than a couple slip-ups.

Through the ups and downs and struggles and withdrawals that followed, she never ceased to give me flashes of why I had fallen for her in the first place. What makes Amber so special is the effortless way she makes the impossible look easy.

Becoming sober together strengthened our relationship in a way the most couples are never lucky enough to experience. We were given the choice to either love each other at our lowest moments or walk away, and we chose love. It peeled back the layers of who we wanted the world and each other to see, and

Karmen   Amber van de Bunt

it exposed us at our most vulnerable. I don't think either of us realized it at the time, but it secured in both of our hearts and minds that the other would never leave our side. Thick and thin, we are there for the other until death do us part.

The gym has always been an important part of my life. I have always been athletic, and as I grew older, the gym replaced the team sports that I had loved and excelled at in my youth. Athletics are my way of expressing myself. The gym serves that same purpose except, it allows me to express a creativity that I haven't experienced before. I can mold my body and mind into what I believe to be my ideal image through hard work. Much like Amber has used performing to express her innermost emotions, I've turned to the gym; it is, after all, much cheaper than a therapist.

In the early days of our relationship, the gym took a back seat to partying and drugs, so what better time to dive back in than when we decided to become sober? Our first trip to the gym was less than successful. She'd snorted Adderall as a sort of preworkout, and we had to turn around because her heart was pounding out of her chest.

When we finally did make it inside and signed her up and got her in the middle of all of the weights and equipment, she took to it like a fish to water, immediately showing an excitement that I had only seen before a night of partying. She was a natural, picking up proper form, reps, sets, and nutrition like it was her first language!

Amber's addictive personality took to planning workouts, prepping meals, and tracking macros. She had taken one terribly destructive addiction and transferred all of that energy into her new addiction: the gym and fitness. Many times, I even found her leading me and teaching me new techniques or theories! It was the perfect replacement for her. To be able to watch her thrive and grow in her love of fitness and lifting and see her take control of her addiction was, and still is, incredible. To this day, working out remains one of our favorite activities to do as a couple.

But, back to porn.

Most people consider porn taboo and even sometimes consider those who make it second-class citizens. On the contrary, I fully believe that what my wife captures on film is beautiful and an incredible form of self-expression. It is a sexy, artistic, athletic expression of one's self. She has found an outlet for all of her pain and struggle and used it to breathe life into this persona of Karmen.

Karmen is a wild, carefree devil. She's animalistic. Just raw sexual aggression, passion, anger. Every emotion in the book thrown into one insatiable and intoxicatingly beautiful woman.

Amber is the girl next door, always down for a laugh or an adventure. She loves her books, crime television, eating stuffed-crust pizza in bed, bubble baths and scented candles.

The two couldn't be more different, but they both need the other. Without one, the other wouldn't exist.

I am her biggest fan and her number one supporter. I never see what she does as dirty or morally wrong. I see a woman who has found a way to make a career out of something that not only is she outstanding at, but that she enjoys as well. And isn't that what we are all looking for in life?

I have never interfered with her career in any way, though we do have a couple of rules regarding certain acts—but those are always subject to her deciding what's best for her scene and what is being asked of her.

The only time that I suggested her maybe going a different direction with her career was when I began to see the mental toll that shooting was taking on her. The longer we were sober, the more I think she began to feel torn between wanting to have a family with me and continuing to shoot. Again, I never told her to quit but instead went with her on the journey to find what was causing her to have these feelings.

I was in Navy boot camp a week and a half before graduation, I believe, when I got a letter from her saying she had shot her last scene and was quitting so we could start a family. The truth is that I cried. I was so happy. But now I realize that it wasn't because she had taken a step back from porn. It was because she had made the choice to figure out and heal from her mental demons, and that was something to be excited about.

Porn will always be a part of us and our marriage. Karmen will always be there. This is the first time I'm actually admitting this: I think that Amber needs Karmen. She's an outlet that she cannot find elsewhere. She is a powerful part of who my wife is, and of course I had never ruled out a comeback. So my answer, when asked about how I feel about her career, is always, "I'm envious. She does something she loves, and she gets paid a lot of money to do so."

Writing this from my berthing on deployment, half a world away from her and our daughter and all that I know; I had to dig down deep in my memories and relive many different emotions. Mostly happy ones, but some sad, scary, and helpless moments as well. I have realized that through loving Amber, my freckle-faced girl next door, I have learned who I really am and learned to love the parts of myself that I never did before. I've learned that nothing I face in my life will ever take me down so long as I have hope.

I am eternally grateful to her for having given me the opportunity to contribute to her memoir. I hope that you have enjoyed this crazy, entertaining, uplifting, frightening, but most of all hopeful story as much as I have enjoyed it. I know that it has made me fall ever deeper in love with her than I ever thought possible.

Acknowledgements

A HUGE THANK YOU first and foremost, to Rare Bird, for publishing my story. Tyson Cornell, for believing in me as a first-time author and giving me the opportunity to share my journey. Guy Intoci, for being the best editor I could've possibly worked with; always making me laugh and making editing fun. A special thanks to Julia Callahan, Hailie Johnson, and Jessica Szuszka for all you've done.

Thank you to my husband, Alex, for being the best support system I could ask for as a sex worker and a wife. You are the type of man that women think don't exist anymore. I consider myself so lucky that you chose me to spend your life with. Thank you for never trying to change me and for always being supportive of my career. And lastly, for not divorcing me when I was a pregnant hormonal crazy monster. You're the real MVP.

Thank you to my dad and sisters for loving me unconditionally. I know my choices in life have not always been easy for you to handle. You are strong and appreciated. I hope I make you proud today.

Thank you to my mother-in-law and father-in-law for welcoming me into your family. You give me inspiration in so many ways. I aspire to always have a strong marriage like yours. I know I can look to both of you when I need guidance and thats something I haven't always had. I love you both so much and appreciate everything you do for me and my family. You are magnificent parents and grandparents.

Thank you to my aunt Paula and grandma Jojo for being mother figures in my life growing up. Your care and presence is always something I am thankful for. Not only did you babysit me frequently while I was growing up, you babysat my daughter for me so I could have time to write this book. I love you both so much.

Thank you to Bria for being the one friend that has never left my side. We may have grown apart and different in many ways but our friendship survives strong. Cheers to us for going from drug addicts with mommy issues to being strong working independent mothers. Thank you for all the times you were there for me—even when you shouldn't of been. You are an astounding human.

Thank you to Marcos Rivera for always making me laugh on set, doing multiple photoshoots for fun with me over the years and for capturing my cover image. Thank you the most for the intense and personal in-depth conversation prior to capturing that image.

A huge thank you to Jennie Ketcham. Your memoir inspired me to finally start writing my own story. When I reached out to you on social media, I was not expecting you to take me under your wing. Your kindness helped me write an outline, edit, and learn how to reach out to publishers. I honestly don't think I would've gotten this far without you.

Thank you to Sandra and Anthony at OC Modeling for being the only agents I've had who cared for me as a person— even when I left the industry.

To the directors and performers who have touched my life in positive ways: Adriana Chechik, Joanna Angel, Ryan Hogan, Michael Woodside, Lela Star, Katrina Jade, Kissa Sins, Megan Rain, Abby Lee Brazil, Nikki Delano, Rob Piper, Ivy Labelle, Prince Yahshua, Jason Luv, August Ames, Kimberly Kendall, Dani Daniels, Asa Akira, Xander Corvus, Jim Camp, Jacky St. James, Vic Lagina, Keiran Lee, Francois Clousot, Jules Jordan, Derek Dozer and Greg Lansky.

Thank you to my social media followers and fans. I read your comments everyday in awe that I have touched your life in some way. Your support and kind words are treasured.

To the readers that picked up this book because you are struggling as well—you got this. It might seem far-fetched that you could ever overcome your battles but if you learn anything from my story, I hope that you learned its possible. I'm always a DM on social media away if you need support.

Saving the best for last, thank you to my daughter, Vienna. Even before you were born you would give me strength to keep on. Just thinking that one day I would have a daughter would give me reason to live. Your name was picked out twelve years before you were even conceived—that's how long I waited for you. I vow to give you the mother-daughter relationship that I never had. You give me so much hope and happiness with just a single smile. You are the goofiest, smartest, most adorable little girl, and I am wholeheartedly obsessed with giving you the life